# Modernity Without a Project

# MODERNITY WITHOUT A PROJECT

Essay on the Void Called Contemporary

C.B. Johnson

punctum books ✸ brooklyn, ny

MODERNITY WITHOUT A PROJECT: ESSAY ON THE VOID CALLED CONTEMPORARY
© C.B. Johnson, 2014.

http://creativecommons.org/licenses/by-nc-nd/3.0/

This work is Open Access, which means that you are free to copy, distribute, display, and perform the work as long as you clearly attribute the work to the authors, that you do not use this work for commercial gain in any form whatsoever, and that you in no way alter, transform, or build upon the work outside of its normal use in academic scholarship without express permission of the author and the publisher of this volume. For any reuse or distribution, you must make clear to others the license terms of this work.

First published in 2014 by
punctum books
Brooklyn, New York
http://punctumbooks.com

punctum books is an independent, open-access publisher dedicated to radically creative modes of intellectual inquiry and writing across a whimsical para-humanities assemblage. We solicit and pimp quixotic, sagely mad engagements with textual thought-bodies. We provide shelters for intellectual vagabonds.

ISBN-13: 978-0692351260
ISBN-10: 0692351264

Cover Image: detail from Superstudio (Frassinelli, Magris Alessandro e Roberto, Toraldo di Francia, Natalini), *The Continuous Monument: New York Extrusion* project. Aerial perspective. 1969. Cover design by Katherine Johnson.

## Table of Contents

—ഝ—

Image Credits

01: Introduction: "The Contemporary" ::   1

02: Modernity without a Project ::   23

03: Remaking the Museum of Modern Art ::   63

04: Complacencies of the New Architecture ::   117

05: Endgame: Consequences of Contemporaneity ::   175

References ::   185

Acknowledgments

# Image Credits

*Figure 1* (Cover/Back Flyleaf). Superstudio (Frassinelli, Magris Alessandro e Roberto, Toraldo di Francia, Natalini), *The Continuous Monument: New York Extrusion* project. Aerial perspective. 1969. Unbuilt. New York, Museum of Modern Art (MoMA). Graphite, color pencil, and cut-and-pasted printed paper on board, 38 x 25-3/4' (96.5 x 65.4 cm). Gift of The Howard Gilman Foundation. © 2014. Digital image, The Museum of Modern Art, New York/Scala, Florence.

*Figure 2.* Alfred Hamilton Barr, Jr. (1902-1981), 'Torpedo' diagrams of the ideal permanent collection of The Museum of Modern Art, as advanced in 1933 (top) and in 1941 (bottom). New York, Museum of Modern Art (MoMA). Prepared by Alfred H. Barr, Jr., for the 'Advis-ory Committee Report on Museum Collections,' 1941. Offset, print-ed in black, 8-1/2 x 11' (20.3 x 29.2 cm). Alfred H. Barr, Jr. Papers, 9a.15. The Museum of Modern Art Archives, NY. MA70. © 2014. Digital image, The Museum of Modern Art, New York/Scala, Florence.

*Figure 3.* Rem Koolhaas (b. 1944), Charrette Submission for The Museum of Modern Art Expansion, New York, NY. Aerial perspective. O.M.A. (Office for Metropolitan Architecture), 1997. New York, Museum of Modern Art (MoMA). Mixed media collage on vellum 11 3/4 x 16 1/2" (29.8 x 41.9 cm). Gift of the architect. © 2014. Digital image, The Museum of Modern Art, New York/Scala, Florence.

*[I]t is time ... to consider some final return or reinvention of the outmoded in full postmodernity, a recurrence that is doubtless the most paradoxical of all since it proves to be the very concept of modernity itself, which we had all naively assumed to be long since superseded. But it is in fact back in business all over the world . . . .*

Fredric Jameson, *A Singular Modernity*

*Most people, me included, are most comfortable conceptually living about ten years back from whatever point in time we've reached. I think we all have these moments that are vertiginous, and terribly exciting, and very frightening, in which we realise the contemporary absolutely. And it induces terror and ecstasy, and we retreat from it because we can't stay in that state of panic, which is the real response to what's happening to us. We're more comfortable with an earlier version of who we were, and what we were, it makes us feel more in control.*

William Gibson, *No Maps for These Territories*

# 01: Introduction
## "THE CONTEMPORARY"

> Contemporary art, sure, but contemporary with what?
> Paul Virilio

No global city today is ideologically complete without an official museum of *contemporary* art, no art is "cutting edge" unless it is *contemporary* art, and no proposed architecture is deemed worthy of construction unless it is *contemporary*. But what does this label, used so authoritatively by today's institutions, mean exactly? Being "contemporary" appears to have become, in the twenty-first century, a new universal right. Communication technologies have driven the present from the temporal divides of modernity toward a condition the anthropologist Marc Augé described as a shared planetary "contemporaneity" of diverse worlds, in which the "parameters of time, like those of space, are changing, and this is an unprecedented revolution" (14). The idea that drives this volume is to resituate the apparently consensual discourse of "the contemporary" within history and thereby see it in a critical light. The emerging view will not be as celebratory as that used by proponents of the phrase. This means boldly reflecting upon the history of modernity and postmodernity, just as these periodising hypotheses are eclipsing after the second millennium.

By way of initial observation, the discourse of "the contemporary"—which is often just used as a shallow synonym for newness—is neither explosive, as was the discourse of modernity, nor melancholy, like the discourse of the postmodern, with its apocalypses and simulacra. It is also not very new. The background of these earlier projects will be instructive in illuminating one of the most ideological aspects of the common occurrence of "the contemporary": its value as a signal of widespread cultural change used to label, and naturalise, the era that succeeds the postmodern. Throughout the ages of modernity and full postmodernity, the word "contemporary" had been used mostly in subordinate fashion to "the modern" and "the postmodern", or in synchrony with these terms, uncritically shifting to the order of the day. It was a subservient term. Only relatively recently did it begin to preoccupy cultural institutions as a central value. The term had not—until about the 1990s—been used to imply that the situation it named was somehow more advanced or unique to the times than that offered by "the modern" and "the postmodern"; these hereby became associated with an old guard. If the modern meant to transcend others in time, and the postmodern meant to transcend the modern itself, then the contemporary means to transcend the modern and the postmodern taken together. Yet, parasitically and arbitrarily, "the contemporary" feeds off the projects of the modern and the postmodern.

The mapping and illustrating of the uses and ideological ramifications of "the contemporary" is in its infancy. This is particularly true in the context of commanding institutions and disciplines invested in giving a sense to the present moment. This volume offers a strong articulation of how "the contemporary" has been used much in the spirit of commentaries on "the modern" and the condition that the poet and essayist Charles Baudelaire, as early as the 1860s, called *modernité*. In "The Painter of Modern Life", Baudelaire used the term to indicate a revolt, an attitude against the classical, the name for an experience unique to metropolitan and industrial life and art. After Baudelaire, "modernity" came to describe not just an attitude against the past and tradition, focused on historic and revolutionary breaks, but the multiplying effects of that attitude on the world; indeed it was extended to describe the whole historical period encompassing the twentieth century's cataclysmic changes, which were technological, social, political, cultural, and aesthetic. Postmodernity—modernity's critical twin or ironic sequel—arose to reflect upon and resist the projects of high modernism that had wrought such breathtaking change by the middle of the century, which projects had so radically brought the future crashing down upon the present. Taken together, these terms, as organising concepts of the present today, have become relatively used up—historical rather than contemporary. Few serious reflections exist on this discursive shift from the postmodern to "the contemporary", which it would be unwise to ignore, given the valuable accumulation of knowledge under the rubrics of modernity and postmodernity. The questions that these movements posed must not be junked with their terms. The junking of the terms is synonymous with the loss of a sense of a different time before ours and a different time after, which is, worryingly, the very loss of our historical context through which progress and projects are judged.

The project to assert a theory of "the contemporary" as an imperative, against uncritical uses of the term, has perhaps most confidently and articulately been put forward by the art historian Terry Smith, who has defined today's issue of historical periodisation as "the contemporaneity question".[1] Smith has posited a concept of "contemporaneity" (modelled on modernity and postmodernity) as the most productive option for providing the basis for a critical theory of the present—as a

---

[1] For an overview of Terry Smith's pathbreaking work on "contemporaneity", see his introduction to the book *Antinomies of Art and Culture* (2008) and numerous essays, including "Contemporary Art and Contemporaneity" (2006a) and "World Picturing in Contemporary Art: Iconogeographic Turning" (2006b).

periodising concept. The selection of the term is strategic; contemporaneity has a "world picturing" function premised on the conceptual infrastructure of Martin Heidegger's essay "The Age of the World Picture".[2] In this context, to periodise in this context is to combat the isolated uses of "the contemporary" and "contemporary art" in the service of rendering a meaningful world, and world picture, for art, architecture, and experience, to function within, or in turn, for art, etc., to alienate.

But this is anything but a stable world picture; rather, for Smith, it acts precisely in its resistance to the old tendencies of modernists who sought to define the world as a whole from their own default (or unconscious) viewpoints, as expressions from the global metropolitan centres, which define the world for others imperialistically. Contemporaneity, then, beyond Heidegger's universalising optimism, is:

> characterized by intense competition between world pictures that claim to be universal but which—conspicuously, and often dangerously—fall short. In so far as it can be taken as a whole, this amounts to a picture of a world in which no encompassing picture of its wholeness is possible. We may well have arrived at a time in human history so immersed in so many temporalities that are so asynchronous, as cultures clash incommensurably, that, despite the instanteity of imaged knowledge of events and places … we cannot picture this as any kind of coherent time, we cannot draw the strings of commensurability together into a recognizable figure. (Smith 2006c: 22)

---

[2] As Heidegger put it, "The expressions 'world picture of the modern age' and 'modern world picture' both mean the same thing and both assume something that could never have been before, namely, a medieval and an ancient world picture. The world picture does not change from an earlier medieval one into a modern one, but rather the fact that the world becomes picture at all is what distinguishes the essence of the modern age" (130).

"Contemporaneity", then, functions as a kind of stand-in figure, a simulacrum, indicating a state succeeding the usefulness of the old grand narrative guards but a state, by definition, ungraspable in its whole.

Although it potentially induces quizzicality at first, this is an enormously useful and suggestive term, in that contemporaneity permits a refreshed critique of the old movements and offers views into the current century's more troubling emergent phenomena, of which the term, and ethos, may indeed be symptom as well as diagnosis. Indeed, the term implies a demand for new studies of all kinds, ranging from redescriptions of old institutions (as they are often acting out their own "redescriptions" in terms of physical rebuilding or renovation), critical descriptions of the new institutions devoted to "the contemporary" (of which the broad network of museums and biennales committed to "contemporary art" are only the most visible), questions to do with time and temporality, questions of break and continuity in history (that are always ideological), and questions of consensual hallucination, to questions of the defining conditions of the present epoch. (This includes the biggest generational issues, from universal climate trouble to the global financial crisis [GFC] that has meant cancelled contemporaneity—because its physical production in museums and architecture demands funding/capital—for many around the globe but has otherwise ramped up the prestige of "the contemporary" where its construction is ongoing.) The term also begs for analyses of architecture as it undergoes redefinition in relation to the vanished postmodern past (seeking to recover a collective sense of being in the contemporary city) and studies of contemporary art, of its internal content but also, most crucially, its institutional framing.[3]

---

[3] The institutional definition of art is largely subscribed to in what follows—the ontological question of what art is shall not be approached here. There are worse places to begin investigation into the issue of art's definition today than Arthur C. Danto's last book, *What*

The flows of "the contemporary" are mapped in what follows in terms of a third phase of modernity that global capitalism is going through. This contemporary modernity, or "contemporaneity" (more radically overcoming what Heidegger called the gigantic in time and space with digital online realities than the philosopher could foresee), has no project in the old sense of Western modernity, except maybe growth itself. The ethos here is in keeping with the one put forward by the philosopher Henri Lefebvre in the early 1960s as the issue presented itself to postwar modernity. Lefebvre summed up the attitude of the day, stating, "passionately accepted or no less passionately rejected, modernity should require no theory" (1)—a sentiment with which he disagreed. Anyone uttering doubt towards the "modern project" was branded, with accompanying shock and horror, as not being "modern". History almost seems to be on repeat concerning today's sense of a right to "the contemporary", or the feeling of a sort of moral obligation towards it, which circulates without critical reflection on what, or whom, is included and excluded by that term. The fact remains that when art, architecture, and so on, are labelled "contemporary", there is still much more to be said. Mass contemporaneousness has been in process for generations, but simply being contemporaneous, by definition, excludes the demand for a non-contemporaneous other time, located in a future different from our eternal now. High modernity, despite its considerable (and at its worst, inhumane) faults, at least knew how to dream of an age ahead on the historical timeline that was different, collectively desirable, and exciting, if hologrammatic at best.

We are then dealing with a periodising proposition; the challenge is to think with it. The era commencing in the 1990s, and intensifying in the 2000s, has consensually junked reference to the modern and the postmodern for "the con-

---

*Art Is* (2013), which proposes, against the grain of "the contemporary", a thesis for art's essence.

temporary". The work to be done in the age of this cultural preference involves a reflective process, a "bid for knowledge" (1), as Lefebvre put it. The historical phase, diverse and still unfolding, is marked by its own aesthetic options and institutions, but while these may look like modernisms or an avant-garde, they are not; at least, not in the traditional sense. The avant-gardes of modernity a hundred years ago operated outside of the institutions. Indeed the institutions had little or no interest in the contemporary as such. Today, whole institutions are devoted to "the contemporary", and occasionally the stamp is even capitalised for extra authoritative effect: The Contemporary. The art of modernity, at its most crucial, meant the negation of art in art's institutions (consider Duchamp, the Futurists, even the Impressionists). In "contemporary" society—global and multicultural—art is not just business but business is the whole of art, and the would-be Utopian tendencies of modernity are redirected into a place invested in cancelling critical potential and managing its energies. The whole discourse from this view is, then, a co-optation or strategy of containment by power, where critique is rendered safer than it ought to be. Or, as Theodor Adorno and Max Horkheimer put it in a different context, these institutions can be said to legitimise a series of "calculated mutations which serve all the more strongly to confirm the validity of the system" (129).

"The contemporary" has a polemical power and induces undying sense of nowness. This, however, will presumably and paradoxically enough, age, wear, and tear, and become used up in time. Indeed, this was classically understood to be the case for modern art in an earlier age. In the early days of the Museum of Modern Art in New York, when the contemporaneity of a painting ceased to be meaningful, the artwork was sold off to the more established Metropolitan Museum, to keep the MoMA fresh or *modern*. The majority of canonical high modern art, antiquated in comparison to today's contemporary art, has found permanent residency in museums or private collections, and is simply no longer available in the global auction house. No doubt the disappearance of art from the market is one of the pressures producing the rise of "the contemporary" paradigm as it is known in the art world. The "story" here begins with a focus on projections of the term itself and seeks to account for its eventually strong role within the twenty-first century version of what Adorno and Horkheimer called the "culture industries" (121) long ago in their classic *Dialectic of Enlightenment*.

Expressed another way, this book pursues, then, no less than the wholly unanticipated loss of the once operative present-tense descriptors that dominated and defined the last century. This is not just a matter of semantics. The modern characterised the last century—that period which Alain Badiou referred to (with reference to the century's reckoning of Utopic visions) as being determined by "the passion for the real" (2007: 2).[4] This was modernity: a time that oversaw vastly different ideological movements all trying to bring their own visions for the future into being, however opposed, ghastly, or desirable. It was the last time that society really believed in a future that was grasped as better than the present. (Which presumably says more about the nature of the present itself at that time than any imagined future as such; Utopian projects are here understood as desperate, radical negations of the present, and as being practical rather than aesthetic.)

The recent custom of "the contemporary" throws into the rear-view mirror the modern, its reaction, the anti-modern, and their quizzical replacement: the postmodern. These terms variously articulate cultural logics, historical periods, and aesthetics. Dropped from view, nothing coherent has been offered to replace such slogans. The latent but powerful claim of "the contemporary" is that it is all we have left—a perpetual present. It is opposed, by definition, to the chronological im-

---

[4] For Badiou, among the twentieth century's originalities is its unification of the real with state crime: the "totalitarian century" (2007: 2).

agination, to great before and after structures of feeling. Indeed, the attitude of "the contemporary" describes a fear of singularity and unification sent out of favour by the ills of high modernist Utopianism. Thus, the contemporary is hesitant in a new way; it is non-committal, with dubious temporality (or at least a different temporality), without an explicit connection to earlier movements. To its subjects, this mode appears to offer a safety zone or suspended time within which one experiences a kind of creative freedom once again. It offers a quick route out of the overburdened, over-historicised and over-theorised paradigms of modernity and postmodernity. This exit, however, is something of a mirage. Upon examination, "the contemporary" can be seen as elitist and rigid in its own way, often concealing order within "openness" and surface change. At its most mainstream or democratic, "the contemporary" appears more like the brutal past that postmodernists thought was outmoded than the future free from oppression that modernists so dearly desired. It might be viewed in this sense as a weird or incoherent restoration of the experience of the high modern. Certainly, it is different, and its difference is cause for celebration, but it is not as different as it wishes to be, and the celebrations are premature (especially when reduced to single works of spectacle or design-fetish architecture).

The weakening and breakage of the postmodern as a "cultural dominant", in Raymond Williams's cultural materialist sense, has opened the way for revaluations of all kinds of essentially modernist emergent cultural phenomena that the reign of postmodernism had "definitively" placed under erasure, particularly aesthetic forms of modernism and design reheated and served up as "contemporary", without curatorial or market flinching. Actual historical modernism is now just "residue" in a museum in terms of reified artistic style if not necessarily in terms of cultural logic. The modern, or high modern, has long become historical, and the postmodern—a strong critique of the excesses of the high modern—has lost much of its critical steam. When not served anachronistically as "contemporary", the latter have also lost their market value (except, arguably, as historical curiosity, and acutely so in the overdeveloped world). The Victoria and Albert Museum in London recently held large exhibitions that offered a rough chronology of the uses of the twentieth century modern, of which postmodernism, as a style, is retrospective. This signalled a return to the discourses of the high modern and the postmodern (as does the existence of their catalogue books, which will exist much longer than the exhibits themselves). These exhibits are big affairs and reveal that the modern and postmodern are not only public and respectable, but are positively chic.[5] They are, however, rendered safe and unthreatening, de-politicised from their historical projects into object fetishism. The V&A curators Glenn Adamson and Jane Pavitt said explicitly that the postmodern is the current age's heritage: "postmodernism stands in relation to our own moment as the Steam Age did to its oil-powered future" (10). When properly historically located in this way, postmodernism was the last pre-digital avant-garde as such.

The contemporary after modernity and postmodernity introduces a difference that lies not simply in the style of the recent "modernisms" most visible in the world of art and the wing of cultural production that is architecture. New versions have been named: Sylvester Okwunodu Ogbechie's "neomodernism" (165–70), Terry Smith's "remodernism" (2006a: 689), and Owen Hatherlay's "pseudomodernism" (xxiv)—these are just some of the varieties. These phenomena, in their full articulations, constitute attempts to return a strong critical content to the otherwise shallow rubric of "the contemporary" by either connecting current trends to a sense of historical continuity or by unmasking the impossibility of modernist revival celebrated in museum exhibitions and the market. Nor

---

[5] Three of these notable exhibitions at the V&A were: "Modernism: Designing a New World: 1914-1939" of 2006; "Cold War Modern: Design 1945-1970" of 2008; and "Postmodernism: Style and Subversion 1970-1990" of 2011.

does the difference lie simply in the new super scale of "the contemporary"; within architecture, for instance, the oversized is made possible not by new technologies so much as by ever larger labour markets. Indeed, whole slave labour cities, as depicted and critiqued by Mike Davis, are organised to produce incredible concentrations of private wealth.

"The contemporary" introduces an attitude that is flexible but superficial and that can be used for whatever ideological or market shifts the day requires. It is offered here that the ubiquitous contemporary is very far from innocent; as the face of globalising capital, its job—however default or unconscious (it is not intentionally sinister, not most of the time)—is to cancel out the capital-unfriendly critical dimensions of the previous movements. Further, I submit that "the contemporary" is a pseudo-concept that requires little analysis in itself. What is needed is its realisation as a narrative category that throws the present back into dialogue with the critical movements of the past, thus demanding the articulation of futures different from the present.[6]

The debate about how "the contemporary" is to be thought about after the reigns of the modern and the postmodern has been coming for some time. The conference "Modernity ≠ Contemporaneity: Antinomies of Art and Culture after the Twentieth Century" in Pittsburgh, Pennsylvania in 2004 marked the advent of what might be called, in the words of Raymond Williams, "conscious contemporaneity".[7]

---

[6] I offer the conversion of concept into narrative as an adaptation of Jameson's reading of the "modern" as a pseudo-concept that demands narration above all else in *A Singular Modernity* (2002), which may indeed be an update of his adage to "Always historicise!"

[7] Raymond Williams made the call that "the period of conscious 'modernism' is ending" (1983: 439) by which he meant a modernism that carried a theory of its own modernity. The period of making it had come and gone; now was the time to live with it, its consequences, its unconscious or default reign, as common sense. The Pittsburgh conference sought to attack and theorise the non-theoretical

It was organised by Terry Smith, Okwui Enwezor, and Nancee Condee, and was opened by Fredric Jameson, whose name is synonymous with an unmasking of the category of postmodernity as "the cultural logic of late capitalism" (1991). The conference was the first very public event that elicited critique of the high modern and the postmodern taken together in the hopeful formation of a critical theory of the present under the rubric of "contemporaneity".[8] This last term, as I have indicated, is intended to suggest that "the contemporary", however paradoxically, has itself become a period, or is the attitude of a period. It presents, counter-intuitively, a *period without end*. The proposal of the conference asked whether the paradigms of modernity and postmodernity and their associated "isms" were still adequate.[9] The conference put forward, among

---

or "unconscious" uses of "the contemporary". It seems to be the fate of *un*periodising terms that they finally collect the thoughts of periodisation.

[8] Most of the papers from this seminal event are available in *Antinomies of Art and Culture*, which is edited by the conference organisers. The papers treat the term and its cognates in many ways—some judgmentally and others in celebratory fashion. The conference was fuelled by the question, "In the aftermath of modernity, and the passing of the postmodern, how are we to know and show what it is to live in the conditions of contemporaneity?" It was also given an urgency by the political contexts of the day—among them (more are noted towards the end of chapter two) the ongoing US occupations in Iraq and Afghanistan, the so-called "war on terror" and its paranoid discourses, and, most immediately, the 2004 re-election of George W. Bush Jr. In the present work I make no attempt to systematically read and situate the papers, diverse in nature, from the conference. Ten years on, the present volume is, however, very much in the spirit of the conference.

[9] Although Jameson opened the event, his paper was situated, as may be expected, within good old postmodernity and globalisation rather than the "bad new things" of contemporaneity. The theorist has maintained that the now of the present moment is a blind spot for those within that moment: "For the present is not yet a historical period: it ought not be able to name itself and characterise its own

other things, a three-part periodisation that is formative of my commentaries in this book, and which I consider more as a myth or story to think upon rather than as a truth statement. The myth organises our thinking into an heroic phase of modernist thought that fetishised progress in the arts, followed by a deconstructive phase of postmodernist thought that appears now as a vanishing mediator to the contemporary, and a reading of the conditions of their aftermaths in terms of a modernism, or, to use Terry Smith's clever but ultimately unsatisfactory pitch, "contemporism"[10] lacking a project, to which end the present moment, and the present system, is falsely stretched to infinity.

All of these terms present large-canvas issues. Presenting them all neatly is not easy, nor is it necessarily desirable. The sociologist Zygmunt Bauman suggested, in a *Thesis Eleven* article, that it is unwise to paint epic canvases during revolutions because they will be torn up (2002: 15). I offer, at the risk of shredding, that contemporaneity has been the key issue within modernity from the beginning (since at least Immanuel Kant and his famous answer to the late eighteenth-century question, "what is enlightenment?") and that each major epoch has characterised its own approach or attitude towards it: modernist, postmodernist, and now a contemporary approach not in synch with the projects of the modern or the postmodern.

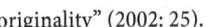

originality" (2002: 25).

[10] "Someone, soon, may baptize it 'contemporism'—a contraction, perhaps of contemporary modernism—or 'remodernism'— emphasising its renovating, recursive character—to predictable scorn followed by eventual acceptance ... Better, perhaps, not to name it: like all unspecifiable but deeply desired values, it is more powerful when taken for granted" (Smith 2006a: 689).

The examination of "contemporaneity" outlined in this book is historical rather than stylistic or anthropological. The genealogical attitude, used here in the tradition of Friedrich Nietzsche's philosophy, comes at the problem not from within the term's internal meaning or content but from the situations in which the term "contemporary", but also its world picturing extension, "contemporaneity", has been used. My intention has been to question the deployment and uses of the term, as opposed to trying to pin down a true and final meaning. This is not, then, a search for essential and eternal definitions—a preoccupation associated with the most traditional or stereotyped philosophy. The aim is not a moral one, in Nietzsche's sense, to decide if it is "good" or "evil". Nor is it to determine whether or not one says "yes" or "no" to the contemporary, in terms of prohibitions or permissions. The aim, in Foucault's sense, is to "account for the fact that it is spoken about, to discover who does the speaking, the positions and viewpoints from which they speak, the institutions which prompt people to speak about it and which store and distribute the things that are said" (1990: 11). This conjoins the Nietzschean aim to account for "the contemporary" as both good *and* evil. To consider what is being lost as well what is to come.

"Genealogy" refers to Nietzsche's work in the 1870s and, almost a hundred years later, to Foucault's appropriation of Nietzsche in his immensely original and highly detailed works that are arguably genealogies. The works of both philosophers were genealogies of those things that have long been thought to have no history, as Foucault stated, such as "sentiments, love, conscience, instincts" (1991: 76). To this list we might add "the contemporary". As will become clear, the binaries of negative and positive, good and evil, and, crucially, the contemporary and the historical are not black and white but of a different order: *they are grey*. I have therefore not sought to write a history in the traditional sense of showing the evolution of an idea, an event, an individual, or institution. If "genealogy is grey", it does not perform a black and white analysis, but a contradictory non-Manichaean approach, that is black *and* white *at the same time*.

The tradition of the genealogy proves to have an affinity with the contemporary itself, or more precisely, genealogy and the contemporary are already bound up in a great tangle. Within genealogical descriptions one is confronted by the incessant rubbing together of the contemporaneity and non-contemporaneity of things. Nietzsche's translator Douglas Smith writes of the Nietzschean genealogy:

> [G]enealogy is at times the record of a search for the roots of a cultural phenomenon, at others the pursuit of its multiple ramifications, the observation of changes in the course of its development, the insistence upon the careful distinctions to be made between the root and the branch, between a tree and its fruit. (1996: xiv)

Contemporaneity is treacherous ground, not least because of its instabilities. One has to try not to fall into the philosophical burrows and an immense modern literature related solely to the philosophical subjects of Time and Temporality, which would require another, different book. (Certainly Peter Osbourne's *The Politics of Time* does attempt something along these lines.) Time does arise in what follows, but the topic is not my object. My "object" is best thought of as the use of a word at a particular moment in its cultural—and, above all, institutional—trajectory. In fact, the issue of time gave definition to modernity; modernity was always about overcoming the present, replacing it with the future tense. In the near-universal capitalist contemporaneity, however, present-tense is the main value. The "contemporary" is then the effect of the ever-renewed zero degree of globally expanding free-market societies.[11]

---

[11] McKenzie Wark put it this way for the artistic context:
> The ideology of the contemporary perpetuates the ideology of the Modern without the latter's claim to a historical vision of progress. Realising that support for the concept of the Modern as

In each part, I have used examples drawn from the archive of the modern and the postmodern in order to mark out the difference that "the contemporary" ushers in; to discover, as it were, the historical edge. The difference, I argue, centres on a version of modernism that looks like modernism but is not modernism, and does not look like postmodernism (but might be). This modernism is expressly without content, in the old sense in which the modern spaced off an ideal world, a set of goals, and a plan for arriving at those goals. Today's "modernism" is a non-teleological or non-goal oriented phenomenon that lacks the critical aspect that was central to the ethical projects of modernity and postmodernity (however internally contradictory and different from one another they may have been).

"The contemporary" is interesting because it still makes judgment but is purposeless within the bigger picture; or, to put it differently, as the philosopher Boris Groys has argued, no longer tries to define its experience in a "project" of modernity or postmodernity. Its attitude is therefore one of hesitation, provisionality, and, as I will suggest, harbours the acceptance that global capitalism's narrative of the free market is the only imaginable collective option for the future.[12]

The inexplicit message from the culture industries of "the contemporary" has been: to be modern today one must be "contemporary". In this way, "the contemporary" has become

> progress offers bourgeois culture as a hostage to historical fortune, the art world obliges with a new idea, the contemporary, as the ever-renewable mask for a new cultural constellation—the eternal bourgeois (360–61).

[12] However, not necessarily to a small extent, the general acceptance of the free market as the only imaginable collective future may finally be changing after the GFC with renewed incredulity arising towards what Marxists call "fictitious capital" (the so-called Occupy Wall Street movement would be one indicator) and the multiple simulacral hangovers of the last decades of the twentieth century in which all that had become air now threatens to turn horrifyingly solid once again (recession, depression, unemployment, etc.).

dominant but remains curiously undefined and functions precisely in its resistance to being pinned down. Depending on your perspective, this is either a healthy diversity or it is uniquely homogenising and suffocating. Groys also noted the qualities of "the contemporary" as it is used in the current age: "the contemporary is actually constituted by doubt, hesitation, uncertainty, indecision—by the need for prolonged reflection, for a delay ... a prolonged, potentially infinite period of delay" (2010: 25–6). The contemporary, then, has, in Groys' view, a different temporality—indeed, atemporality—to that of the earlier movements of modern thought and feeling. It is, then, (depending on your viewpoint), freeing and exciting or deeply conservative and utterly reduced to an impoverished present without a future.

Unlike the modern, which purposed a plan, and the postmodern, which was motivated by scepticism towards the modern project, the consensual discourse of "the contemporary" marks a move into an almost association-free territory, an exit from modernity and postmodernity. This exit, however, is deceptive, and reconstructions of the contemporary are needed that resituate the discourse within historical time. It is a return to historical time that undoes the cultural work already performed by the simulacral ubiquity of "the contemporary". This reading, if it is successful, will capture a sense of the contingency of the present, of its original discursive construction, but also illustrate how it is embedded within the ongoing metanarratives of the present that defined the twentieth century, and that, to no small extent, define the twenty-first.

Now is the time to say something about the money crash at the end of this last decade. The crash has not eliminated or minimised the meaning of "the contemporary" as such, but thrown its prestige into relief. New arrivals of "the contemporary" only serve to ramp up its value, to render it elite. The cancelling of developments heralds the onset of "non-contemporaneity" (a term I borrow from the Frankfurt School theorist Ernst Bloch from his under-appreciated *Heritage of*

*Our Times*, written, appropriately enough, in the 1930s: a wholly dystopian age if ever there was one). This latter is undesirable for it signals an end to growth, lessened connectivity, and even the threat of dishonourable de-linking (look at the recent history of the euro and Greece). Those that have ongoing construction and maintenance of "the contemporary" now enjoy the elitism that comes with possession of scarce goods, which is, of course, the history of bourgeois art collecting and class society itself. "The contemporary" now signals one's access (or lack thereof) to contemporaneity, which is in fact an expression of a new international division of wealth.

To repeat Fredric Jameson's essentially Marxist thesis, the discursive shift away from modern and postmodern to the rampant "contemporary" has been achieved by the "cultural logic of late capitalism" whereby their use-values have been used up for time being—perhaps forever. In a polemic mode, we may have moved to a place beyond even this state of affairs, in a provisional post-late capitalist era (an era of intensified, digital, or light-speed capitalism). The theorist McKenzie Wark suggested we may need to give up on "post" this and "late" that and begin to speak of "early" something else emerging from the old contradictions.[13] This "early something else" era belongs less to a culture of postmodernity than one of sheer, ever-renewed and reloaded contemporaneity; this is not a sustainable contemporaneity, but one living *at the expense of the future*. The most determining issues of the last decade, namely the American wars in Iraq and Afghanistan, global warming, the international oil crises, and the waves of economic uncertainty bring this point home. Postmodernity was parasitic, possessed by a frame of reference to modernity—that progressive (albeit bourgeois) age that laid the deep historical conditions for the current crises and opportunities.

---

[13] McKenzie Wark: "Perhaps it is not late capitalism that ails us, but a whole new stage, emerging out of the contradictions of the last. Perhaps our diagnosis can move on from 'post' this and 'late' that to 'early' something else" (348).

"The contemporary", at its most public level, almost subsumed by the degraded rhetoric of marketing and advertising, has seen the lexical reference severed once and for all. If Renato Poggioli's insight is true, that, "language is our greatest historical revealer" (17), then this presence of a new name indicates the presence of another phenomenon. This phenomenon demands analysis in itself. There has been a change in the way things are done, organised, and thought about with the rise of near-instantaneity, as suggested by Augé, but it may not be a change for the better; or, at least, the change is incomplete.

Jürgen Habermas' enlightenment defence in "Modernity: An Incomplete Project" grasped sites of creativity as among the first to signal critical new states of awareness that are generally of importance to culture; the artistic wing of high modernism showed new possible ways of being and doing, some of which pre-empted the actual world of tomorrow: the Future. The philosopher also called for the project of modernity—an extension of the eighteenth century enlightenment—to be extended into the twenty-first century, not abandoned for a postmodern view disentangled from metanarratives of freedom and progress; the latter abandonment of which had consequences of radical fragmentation and schizophrenia, the experience of life lived without a project. More recently, Groys has put forward something of an extension of this idea into contemporary art studies, recalling that to be "modern" in its time meant understanding one's life and art as experienced and made within a project, often grasped in modernism as abolishing the past to begin a different future. Groys' work translates this ethos into "the contemporary". To simplify, no project is equal to no relationship with time and temporality as such: that is, a reduction to the narrowest vision of the here and now and the merely existing.[14] For Groys, artists and sci-

---

[14] See Boris Groys's work in the essays "Comrades in Time" (2010), "The Topology of Contemporary Art" (2008), and also "The Loneli-

entists offer strong models to the rest of society for how to imagine life as lived within a project; the artist and the scientist both depart from present reality, drop out of common experience as it were, to commit to a future that may not come to pass.

The "contemporary" paradigm in art is in continuity with the high modern in the sense that creativity appears to be the central value, but only when located in relation to refusing a sense of "advanced" time, of being ahead of others in time (the one foot in the future of modernism). The "correct" experience of time, then, ought to be in its simultaneity with others—a sort of egalitarianism of temporality. In this it is in keeping with straightforward breakdowns of the meaning of the word con-temporary—where the Latin *con* means "with" or "together" and the Latin *tempus* or *temporus* means "time". Still, this definition does not do justice to the complexities of the term's use in culture, which is not always matched to the institutions that marshal meanings. What is left to observe after the great studies of the modern and the postmodern is the emergence of the void called "contemporary" that, on the one hand, stalls or shuts out the projects of modernity, and on the other, generates ongoing problems and sites of struggle over meanings. It is also not necessarily anything to be solved; it has an enlightenment value of always making us renew the question of who we are. The examples and studies put forward in the following pages are not exhaustive. This book could be extended further to accommodate the full global reach of the term's construction, to uncover the tacit acceptance of the global in the contemporary, its universalising tendencies, its fantasies of borderlessness, and other moments in its contradictory history. There are many aspects to "the contemporary" that will only be lightly touched on in this book, but I hope to provoke an awareness of the ongoing ideological deployments of the term (as these shift around) and expose

ness of the Project" (2002), where the philosopher reflects upon the value of failed projects.

some of its smug satisfactions.

This book is organised into five chapters. A warning to the reader: Chapter Two is especially theory heavy, but thereafter the chapters are focused around case studies of institutions and individual works of architecture. The final chapter draws some provisional conclusions.

One will notice that New York and the Museum of Modern Art receive more attention than anywhere else. This has to do with the waning of the modern and continued refusal of the postmodern in that institution. (At any rate, chapter three is devoted to this.) But I am also arguing that no matter where we are—the US, the UAE, the UK, the EU, China, Japan, Venezuela, Australia—each of these places deploys "the contemporary" in a context, however imagined, of *belonging*. Belonging, that is, to the same present as opposed to the backwards and forwards temporalities characteristic of modernity—indeed, of imperialism with its production of "unmodern" and "primitive" others. Recall, in modernity, the futurist and often fascist projects to match with economies that seemed to be living in the high modern future: Italy and Russia around a hundred years ago, for instance, or the "Utopian" totalitarian projects based on speeding up to overtake the present of others, in the examples of Germany under National Socialism or China under the Cultural Revolution, with atrocious consequences. "The contemporary" is associated with capitalist economies after the end of the Cold War and the Soviet Empire. The name denotes a Fukuyamen[15] collective hallucina-

---

[15] In a nutshell, Francis Fukuyama notoriously declared in *The End of History and the Last Man* (1992) that a remarkable consensus for liberal democratic hegemony was the final alternative to systems of hereditary monarchy, fascism, and socialism, etc., which was reason to believe that history as defined by struggle for social alternatives

tion of global capitalism without alternatives.

One can appreciate the impossibility of accounting for all of the issues raised here in a short book. The critical description of culture through the lens of the problematic of "contemporaneity" is, then, a collective exercise in which no particular artist, theorist, or commentator is positioned to have a monopoly. It is the spirit of this book to seek to frame the questions around "the contemporary" in new ways. As noted, the charge that the whole territory and its individual elements are messy and ambiguous is correct; it is the Nietzschean genealogy as an approach that allows for these elements to be presented and stored in their elusiveness, which is how I begin this critique of millennium tendencies that look modernist, but are not, and go by the name "contemporary".

had ended. The notion that "the contemporary" relieves us of the issues facing the modern and the postmodern might be the art world's equivalent illusion.

## 02: Modernity without a Project

> The "contemporary" is a cultural élite ... So the "contemporary" has nothing to do with time, nor with age.
> 
> Wyndham Lewis

The broadest terms in circulation under the sophisticated consumerism of high culture today present us with a mystifying situation. At the turn of the century "the contemporary" underwent discursive unrest, becoming one of the most favoured, uncritically promoted and celebrated cultural paradigms. The paradigm of "the contemporary" is used at the most public level to explain away and apologise for any number of expansions and renovations in the arts. On the other side of the dial, demolition in architecture is the new open secret order of the day, according to Franco La Cecla, with the emergence of a whole commercial explosives demolition industry (the leading North American company of which even claims that demolition is an art form).[1] No doubt, this charged

---

[1] Controlled Demolition, Inc. has finally commodified the tabula rasa. See Franco La Cecla's discussions of demolition in *Against Architecture* (2012) where he charges that, especially in the world of mass housing, "Today there is demolition; it is its great moment" (70).

phrase—"the contemporary"—has performed significant ideological work in other sectors as well, outside of art, museums, architecture, cities, urban production, and subject formation, where it has been used to usher in change.[2] For better or worse, the themes here are art and representation, which are in their own ways about the world we live in.

Not unlike "the modern" in its heyday, the term registers a knowing, often antagonistic, break from the past, which is seen as outmoded and soon to be forgotten. We are henceforth in endlessly paradoxical territory, and not least because the paradigms that the contemporary wishes to displace—the modern, the postmodern—were themselves performers of this kind of function, albeit under different historical, geographic, cultural, and aesthetic conditions. If the modern and the postmodern were movements within history that projected themselves into a vision of the non-contemporaneous, "the contemporary" introduces itself as a kind of anti-movement; once one has reached the contemporary, where is left to go?

It will be instructive—and hopefully estranging, in the Brechtian sense—to mark out the disseminations of this cultural premise that has no less than reconfigured our collective cultural perceptions. This chapter maps a big-picture *historicisation* of the advent of Western culture's use of "the contemporary" and offers a critical diagnosis of the term. The old categories of "the modern" and "the postmodern" once had great force and power, and tended to divide parties at the mention of their names. In the course of the unrest of "the contemporary", however, these terms have been left to dwindle into archaisms. Within critical debates the modern and the postmodern maintain their rigour, but outside of these debates, and specifically within cultural institutions, they are

---

[2] Think, for instance, of contemporary finance (the disappearance of money, commodification of futures); contemporary television (downloadable, flexible); and contemporary security (ramped up state control, xenophobia). Doubtless, the reader can furnish further examples.

treated incredulously—with an air of suspicion, fear, and ignorance. Or, they are simply treated with undue prestige (intended, no doubt, to glorify certain institutions or individual owners and generate mere property value, which has been especially the case in recent years with the category of "the modern").

The modern and the postmodern are often too hastily sketched as movements or thrusts toward a collective meaning, and both are now also understood as historical periods. This is, for the most part, true. The real issue is the characterisation of the profound double aftermath of these world-historical movements, different as they are. Which elements are we clinging onto, whose ideas have been revitalised, and what is being lost, perhaps irrecoverably? It is tempting to buy into the inclusive, open self-image of the aftermath and see not a unified discourse, but a lack of agreement or consensus. The bigger picture sends another signal; however, the current phase of "the contemporary", which to be properly understood must be identified with the expansive historical success of global capitalism and its conditions of possibility (broadly post-USSR), is marked by excessive agreement about the nature of cultural phenomena and the direction of history. The much-ridiculed Fukayamen propaganda about the "end of history" seems to have disturbingly found its home in the sheer proliferation and near-universal acceptance of contemporaneity.[3]

---

[3] Terry Smith has used resources at the Getty Institute in Los Angeles and the University of Pittsburgh to trace the increasing quantitative decline of the term "modern" as a descriptor for current art after the 1960s, and the rise of "contemporary". Smith has traced the "occurrence, and contextual denotation ... along with their deployment in the naming of visual arts museums, galleries, and departments of museums and auction houses, in the major European languages from the 1870s until now". The 1960s are an interesting case in point because at this time "modern" and "contemporary" become interchangeable terms, used with similar frequency and for the same kind

The historical occurrences of "the contemporary" in the fine arts in fact go back a long way, and turn out to be more complicated and tied up within political imaginaries than superficial uses of the term by today's cultural industries imply; the latter rely on the term's surface neutrality and seeming inclusivity (overall, a correctness; that is, what could be less offensive, or more incontrovertible, than being "contemporary"?), and its unique capacity to absorb almost any content whatsoever, *without changing the system*. This chapter casts its net wide over multiple, but not exhaustive, uses of the term from a range of sources, with a view to casting a familiar territory as alien once again.

## THE PRE-CONTEMPORARY CONTEMPORARY

After the Second World War, the world had undeniably become a different place. The succeeding ideological atmosphere in the United States was that of the binary illusions of the Cold War,[4] which seeped into aspects of art and museum culture as much as the political simulacrum, the media, and everyday life. What the institutions do with language gives us some idea of how they imagine the world, à la Wittgenstein's dictum, "To imagine a language is to imagine a world" (qtd. in Perloff 2002: 6). One of the most indicative, if marginal and

---

of artefacts. "Modern", however, declines each subsequent decade after the 1960s: "by approximately 45% into the 1970s, after which it diminishes to a point where, during the 1980s, it virtually disappears as an indicator for the art of the time". Meanwhile, the term "contemporary", which before the 1920s and 1930s was rarely and randomly used, increases in usage by approximately eighty percent each decade after the 1960s. These statistics come from Terry Smith, whom I thank.

[4] Susan Buck-Morss provocatively argued in *Dreamworld and Catastrophe* that the systems in East and West of this era were in fact closely related versions of modernity; notably, that of Soviet Communism having a tendency to mirror its capitalist opposition rather than reveal new and desirable forms of social being.

under-discussed, institutional shifts in usage of the terms "modern" and "contemporary" is to be found in Boston in the late 1940s at the Institute of Modern Art (IMA). This significant cultural-terminological shift was, however, not a revolutionary move, but an attempt to co-opt a version of the modern that had been monopolised by New York's Museum of Modern Art, paving the way for the contemporary art institutes of the latter part of the twentieth century. The institutional break away from a certain construction of "the modern" set the tone (in terms of illustrating a different use of the same thing) not just for the contemporary, but also for the postmodern that was to flourish in the following decades. At this time, however, "the contemporary" was used to signal something different from the twenty-first century version: a step back towards a depoliticised art, a weak modernism.

The Institute of Modern Art was established in 1936 in Boston and became a place of renown, contributing to, rather than challenging, the discursive construction of "the modern" in America. However, in 1948 the IMA deemed modernism to have gone too far, especially in its abstract expressionist mode promoted (or constructed) by Clement Greenberg and the MoMA in New York. Modernism was understood to have lost its standards. The IMA, a conservative institution, supported the Truman Doctrine against communism, and the institute issued a statement of policy announcing its dissatisfaction with the direction of "modern", citing Jackson Pollock (with his abstract, large canvas action paintings) and Arshile Gorky (with his automatic, abstract gestural paintings in bright contrasting colours) as extremists.

Under director James S. Plaut, the institute's people proposed a name change to combat the confusion and bewilderment that Modern Art had created. The institute no longer wanted to be associated with the modern, and would seek, instead, to construct a cultural frame for the *contemporary*. From February 1948 onwards, it would be called the Institute of Contemporary Art (ICA). The term "contemporary", the institute argued, was not contaminated by the "odour" that

Modern Art had become. Modern Art became a term synonymous with "unintelligibility" and "sham", while contemporary, as yet untainted, was deployed as neutral; it promised to restart the display of the art of the time, proclaiming "standards of excellence", with the aim of distinguishing the "good art from the bad, the sincere from the sham". As the *New York Times* made clear in 1948, the new ICA wanted to recognise lexically that "the creative artist remains ahead of his time" (Louchheim 1948: Sec. 2:8). The term "contemporary" was also free of communistic association, which, at the beginning of the Cold War, would have been a political disadvantage for the institute. Pablo Picasso was perhaps the highest profile modern painter to have been publicly self-identified with the communist project, and given the status of that artist in the New York MoMA's collection, MoMA could easily have been identified as a soft patron of communism.

"The contemporary" emerged at this point out of resentment. It is difficult not to read this development as a statement of envy from an institution that was having trouble competing with the New York artistic avant-garde and the MoMA in particular, which had been almost single-handedly inaugurating a new style of modernism with each successive major exhibition: Machine Art followed by the International Style followed by a Frank Lloyd Wright retrospective, and so on, to triumphal post-war Abstract Expressionism. In a sense, for Boston, "the contemporary" was a shallow marketing move, an attempt to retain a strong identity under the looming threat of obsolescence. The contemporary at mid-century was not a revolutionary move, but a step sideways. The force field of the New undeniably remained at the MoMA. This would be the case until the superseding of modern art by official "contemporary art" in the 1980s and 1990s. In the 2000s, Yoshio Taniguchi and Glenn D. Lowry would collaborate to introduce "the contemporary" as an organising principle for the MoMA (which is discussed further in chapter three). For Boston, the narrative of instituting the contemporary found its apex as late as 2006, when the ICA shut down its old headquarters and reopened in a new purpose-built museum on the

Charles River (designed by Diller Scofidio + Renfro), conforming to the dominant paradigm it historically helped to form rather than challenging it. The ICA's new building (against the tropes of the postmodern) reinvigorates a language of high modern form. In *The Art-Architecture Complex*, Hal Foster even went so far as to call it a "neo-Miesian pavilion" (88), emphasising a certain deployment of "the contemporary" as the signal term for an imagined return to modernism beyond the postmodern moment.

We have here a disjunction in the very fabric of what constitutes modernism, or rather an *escape* from it. The term "event" perhaps makes the ICA's late 1940s historic terminological jump sound more momentous than it was: a subtle shifting of ideological emphasis rather than a massive departure from the projects of modernism. It was a mid-century conflict of interpretations that will help to illustrate the legitimate history of "the contemporary" and its appearances throughout the century as a descriptor for artistic culture that consciously tried to shake the pile of overtones accrued by the "modern". All terms become used up eventually, as a single word simply can only hold so much history and accumulation of energy and events. Modern art had, by mid-century, become riddled with notorious associations in America, the most evocative of the time being President Harry Truman's, as noted by Serge Guilbaut: "Truman, the 'new liberal', reacted to modern art as the 'last of the Donderoes' (George Dondero was the notorious senator from Michigan who made the equation 'modern art equals communism' famous)" (1985: 4).[5]

---

[5] The full quotation is instructive for its pointing to the unevenness of the term, which had become as multifaceted as the Cubist paintings it was often used to refer to:

> The true force of the historical contradiction comes into play. Truman, the "new liberal", reacted to modern art as the "last of the Donderoes" (George Dondero was the notorious senator from Michigan who made the equation "modern art equals

The identification of modern art with communism and the Soviets, however inaccurate,[6] brought the modern into the discourse of the Cold War. The term modern at mid-century was suddenly replaced by "contemporary" and used to signify something purer than modern. It signified a reformed modern art, a return to decency, away from the runaway tendencies of the abstraction then currently promoted by the New York Museum of Modern Art. The National Socialist attempt—after the abrupt shutdown of the Bauhaus in 1933—to discredit the modern might again be registered at this point for its rebranding of modern art as *Entartete Kunst*, or "degenerate art", in the 1937 exhibition in Munich of that name.[7] These disparate reactionary examples represent external, political attempts to control the meaning of the modern. Both played a role in discrediting the modern, and hinted at the future dominion of "the contemporary" as an open field suitable for resignification by the next generation.

In the case of the Boston IMA, contemporary was deployed in opposition to modern, and precedes the later, more critically notorious, postmodern (in art discourse ranging from Pop Art in Britain to the US, and onward). The terminological shift in Boston was a belated reaction against *The International Exhibition of Modern Art* or "Armory Show" that had presented the most experimental in European art, from Ingres to the Cubists and, most important, Duchamp's *Nude Descending a Staircase No. 2* in New York in 1913. The show

communism" famous), but under his administration the United States Information Service and the Museum of Modern Art, as early as 1947, began to promote avant-garde art. (Guilbaut 1985: 4)

[6] The Soviets had little use for abstraction by mid-century, as they favoured Socialist Realism: Stalin's official art.

[7] *Entartete Kunst* was, interestingly, one of the most widely attended art exhibitions in German history. It was, despite its manifest anti-modern curatorial content, a chance for the German masses to witness "so-called modern art" first hand. It is likely that many enjoyed the new art, but it was dangerous to contradict the regime.

was legendary for not only attracting immense crowds to look at modern art, but, as the *New York Times* reminisced in 1948, "Indignation meetings were held; friends became enemies; academicians were outraged. Ridicule and valiant praise rose in a controversy which spilled over into the press" (Louchheim 1948: Sec. 2:8). The Armory Show was still exhibiting modernity in its heroic phase. Boston illustrates for us an early scepticism, but still maintains high art as a value—though not necessarily as part of a narrative of advancement.[8]

It was no accident that ridicule centred on Marcel Duchamp's work. In the story of Contemporary Art, Duchamp would return as the historical artist responsible for the most significant—some would say destructive, others liberating— work of modernity: the point of no return. *Fountain* of 1917 was a readymade, store-bought porcelain urinal signed by Duchamp under the pseudonym R. Mutt. This work prepared

---

[8] True to the heroic intention of high modernism, the Armory Show was a scandal for bourgeois Americans, and no doubt contributed to the conservative view that modern art and communism were involved in a single narrative of a transvaluation of values. From the tone of the newspaper's writing of the event in the 1940s, it is evident that the show had become legendary by mid-century and was now integrated as part of the mythos of modern American cultural life, as pathbreaking as Stravinsky's inaugural performance of his *Rite of Spring* in Paris in 1912. In New York, insults abounded: one critic denounced Cézanne for not having learnt his trade properly. For another critic, Hartley had contributed to the "total destruction" of the art of painting. Marin's "Woolworth Building" gave another critic "vertigo", and to another, Matisse was positively "epileptic" (which was of course bad). It was *the* classic moment of the shock of the new in America. But above all, Cubism provoked the most incredulity, the most quizzicality, the most difficulty to the establishment, and Marcel Duchamp's *Nude Descending a Staircase* No. 2 was the *succes de scandale*. "This experiment of presenting similar successive aspects of objects in motion was so baffling that *Art News* offered a $10 prize for the best fifty-word description of the location of the nude and the stairs" (*NYT* 1947: 8).

the way for helping to legitimate what Arthur Danto would call the "transfiguration of the commonplace", or the "adoration of the ordinary" (1997: 128). The latter gained momentum in 1960s Pop Art: the first of many critiques from mid-century modernist abstraction. The moment when the everyday and the banal suddenly shift place to become high art remains an essential reference for all works that seek to radically unsettle categories. It is a flash forward to what Hal Foster later called the "paradigm-of-no-paradigm" (2003: 128), or, following the Italian philosopher Mario Perniola, the era of the enigma in which we are experiencing a limit that is not necessarily meant to be overcome.

The paradigm of aesthetic contemporaneity in our twenty-first century context is unimaginable without reference to Duchamp. But in Duchamp's time his aesthetic was revolutionary: a breakthrough into the "New World" and the attitude of modernity as anti-art, of the commodification of art and profound reallocation of perception. In our contemporaneity, however, Duchamp's revolution has become general art museum culture. Visitors to "the contemporary" have come to expect works that overturn established categories and they are not surprised by the incorporation of art, of any type, by the market; the rejection of public taste and promotion of squalor are valued (as seen in the Young British Art phenomenon of the 1990s). This is the cultural logic of successful revolutions, where the vanguard of the few becomes the everyday of the many. In Jameson's terms, we could say that the break has become a period, which thereby lays the conditions for ever-new and profound breaks or slippages (Jameson 2002: 29 – 30). The fate of the Armory Show is instructive (at least nominally) because, as of 1999, it too has become a commoditised part of the establishment like "the contemporary". Since that year, its name has been annually redeployed in New York to provide a now-respectable historical aura to an international exhibition of dealers of "contemporary art".

In recent times, a shift in terms has not been a powerful enough statement—as signalled by the example of Diller Scofidio + Renfro's ICA—and museums have instead opted for architectural expansion and financial speculation. It is less an intellectual debate or "anticipatory power of meaning" than what Foucault called the "hazardous play of dominations" that—in this case—is primarily economic (1991b: 83). The most contemporary museums are becoming those with the necessary capital needed to name and back the concept. The deployment of architecture has also replaced the once primary purchase of art itself, which has become secondary to the creation of new buildings and ever more elaborate ways of displaying art. "Expansion introduces competition between museums themselves", as Julian Stallabrass argued in *Art Incorporated*, "so that staying the same while all around are growing does not seem an attractive option" (2004: 141). The ICA was the first from-scratch museum to be built in Boston in over a hundred years; over fifty years later, this still stands as a sign of the strength of "the contemporary". In this picture, "the contemporary" has moved from anti-modern strategy to the shining celebratory centre of major business expansion.

## POSTWAR DISJUNCTIONS

The replacement of modern by contemporary was not an all-encompassing phenomenon until our own time. Before "the contemporary" became the dominant consensual hallucination of meaning for people in the arts (a term too often used to avoid theorising and politicising, because of its seemingly politically correct inclusivity and appearance as non-theoretical and non-threatening), heated debates about anti-modernity and postmodernity arose with great force, as well as a revival of high modern Utopianism, especially in the 1960s. An era of profound unevenness followed the Second World War, resulting in a cultural paradigm that characterised itself as having no central paradigm (and therefore no program and no content). It can be described as a period of information disorder. The late 1950s and 1960s—the time that Fredric Jameson, in his intervention *Postmodernism*, argued was marked by a radical cultural break or *coupure* (1991)—

was a starting point for the radical conceptual disjunctions that followed. That it is not possible to deal in clear-cut definitions becomes increasingly clear when one begins to think about the distinctive features of the modern and the contemporary, and the associated variations, partners, and relatives of these terms. The instability of the terms can be grasped as a historical openness to process rather than the seeking of finished, *metaphysical* forms. The unified modern attitude toward the issue of contemporaneity dissipates in this time, replaced by the confusing scene between the wholesale sceptical deconstructions of the postmodernists and the all-consuming disillusionment of default contemporaneity.

Jameson has argued that "modernities" became so common in the late 1950s and 1960s that it seemed superfluous to continue using that term at all. He proposed the postmodern as a periodising hypothesis. The coinage of the word, but not Jameson's provocative meaning, is said to have been the work of the American poet Charles Olsen in a letter to his fellow American poet Robert Creeley, on October 20, 1951—poets may like to be exact in these matters (Hoover, 1994: xxv). It was in, and after, the postmodern moment that we tended to comfortably imagine, in the safety of retrospect, that the terms of the modern made up a unified whole. This observation amounts to a uniform, anti-modernist rejection of that whole. Clement Greenberg's widely adopted coinage of the term "modernism" after the Second World War is a case in point because of the neat packaging effect of retrospect, which avoids the vulgar difficulties of describing one's own present. Postmodernism was, in a sense, the final working through of the long historical impact of modernity—the consequences of modernity.

In Jameson's terms, the postmodern was characterised in large part by the "waning of affect" of the great discourse of modernity (1991: 10). It is in our own time, in a culture uncritically hallucinating "the contemporary", that we are witness to a similar fate of the once-prominent discourse of the postmodern itself, of *its* waning as the most influential attempt to grasp the present historically. To repeat Jameson's terms, we are still very much "in an age that has forgotten how to think historically in the first place" (1991: ix). This is, in a strange way, to cycle Jameson's critique back on itself. He had already done as much in *A Singular Modernity* by acknowledging the slowing of the postmodern's momentum and the "revival" of the concept of modernity:

> Consider some final return or reinvention of the outmoded in full postmodernity, a recurrence that is doubtless the most paradoxical of all since it proves to be that of the very concept of modernity as such, which we had all naively assumed long since to be superseded ... But it is in fact back in business all over the world, and virtually inescapable in political discussions from Latin America to China, not to speak of the former Second World itself ... What purpose can the revival of the slogan 'modernity' still serve, after the thoroughgoing removal of the modern from all the shelves and shop windows, its retirement from the media, and the obedient demodernification of all but a few cantankerous and self-avowedly saurian intellectuals? (2002: 6–7)

This is an unbelievably loaded statement from the theorist whose work has perhaps done the most to shape debate around the issue of postmodernity. Jameson sees the deployment of the modern within the last two or three decades as a substitute for the more critically consequential terms of the postmodern that more correctly allow him to speak of, know, and confront the present. For Jameson, the modern and modernity are nostalgic and ideological, used to *prevent* certain critical diagnoses to do with the aftermath of modernity.

An influential institutional deployment of the "Modern" as a stand-in for contemporary occurred in London at the turn of the century. When the Tate Modern opened in the year 2000 (now one of three Tate franchises, all in the UK), Modern was deployed in place of the more current "contemporary". The establishment did not call this major development Tate Contemporary. No doubt the term was considered and abandoned. Postmodern would have been jettisoned as well, but probably with more ease.

The critic John Rajchman's argument is that the modern and the postmodern have both failed, that the modern is completely antiquated and the postmodern really cannot sensibly apply outside of the 1980s. Likewise, Terry Smith dismissed postmodernism in "The Contemporaneity Question" as a "one-generation wonder", along with "the isolation of postmodernity as a fate of the West ... but not the world" (2008: 6). The relationship between contemporaneity and modernity and modernism is provisional and uncertain. It is certain, however, that these older concepts have more market value than their "post" prefixed counterparts popular in the 1980s and 1990s. The contemporary is a deployment that has exited from a direct reference to the modern, at least by name, which counts for something at the collective level of the consciousness of the age. "Postmodern" maintained a reference to the transformation of everyday life that was the arrival of historic or first-wave modernity aimed at revolution and a radically different world of tomorrow; "the contemporary" possesses a narrower vision. More positively, it is of course possible that the contemporary and contemporaneity prepare the way for a moment of modernism to come—one that could not emerge at the self-conscious and self-critical stage of Western culture that was the postmodern.[9]

---

[9] The poetry critic Marjorie Perloff has suggested in her manifesto *21ˢᵗ-Century Modernism* that the full fruition of the avant-garde "first wave" of modernist experimentation, in poetics, is only now arriving. The American L=A=N=G=U=A=G=E poets, in her authoritative estimation, began the restoration in the 1970s and 1980s. The second generation of Language oriented poets, which is more dispersed than the first generation, is developing the materialist heritage of four early modernists—Duchamp, Eliot, Velimir Khlebnikov, and Gertrude Stein (among others)—in unpredictable directions. In Perloff's vigorous argument, the first wave of revolutionary modernism was cut short by the two wars and the totalitarian regimes of twentieth

The success of postmodernist critique has equalled the wide acceptance that we are in an age of postmodernity. This is less an age than a condition, which was the term used by Jean-Francois Lyotard, the philosopher who may arguably be credited with having provided the term with its most used intellectual meaning: namely, the condition of the "incredulity toward" (Lyotard) or "waning" (Jameson) of metanarratives (the nation state, the West, the party, the proletariat, the Enlightenment project itself, etc.). The condition of postmodernity remains notable for its nominal reference to modernity; it was *part* of the modern. Lyotard argued specifically for the disappearance of metanarratives. Jameson, however, argued contrarily that it may be a case of the provisional burying of master narratives, "their passage underground as it were, their continuing but now *unconscious* effectivity … what I have elsewhere called our 'political unconscious'" (1984: xii). This line of thought suggests a basis for grasping the recent unrest in which the slogans of the modern and the postmodern may become unfashionable or depoliticised but do not easily disappear—they travel or are forced underground, where they retain their energy in the collective unconscious, and their unfortunate surface level expression becomes that of fetish, fad, kitsch, or the occasional eccentric outburst. As suggested in Boris Groys' writing, the big generational and collective

century Europe. (Between the wars, she argues, it seems as if "poems and artworks made a conscious effort to repress the technological and formal inventions of modernism at its origins" [3].) Second wave modernism represents less a revolution than restoration of the original projects. Perloff cites Susan Howe, Charles Bernstein, Lyn Hejinian, and Steve McCaffrey as no more than a prolegomenon of the strength of the big second wave, set off dramatically against the conservative, virtually pre-modern laureate poetry of today, promoted by such publications (where they do give space to poetry at all) as *The New York Times Book Review* and *Times Literary Supplement*. Contemporaneity for Perloff is a chance to restore and take to new heights the original modernist breakthroughs.

projects are buried along with these slogans, so that remaining projects are reduced to those of the status of the individual artist or scientist (or studio or small team); their commitment limited to a non-contemporaneous time, to living briefly, experimentally and imaginatively, in a future that may never come to pass, and indeed in a project that may never even be funded.

Is it, then, that "the contemporary" is the ideological condition of our epoch of global capitalism? If so, it would be theoretically consistent with the way in which the modern—which was not a period, but a way of referring to the present—*became* one through the lens of "modernity". "The contemporary", which is similarly thought of as a resistance to periodisation, can be rethought as a period through the anti-totalizing category of contemporaneity. Certainly, "the contemporary" has been around in common usage long enough to accumulate some wear, troublesome inflection, and history. The term can be charged with having become historical, but not yet retrospective, not yet nostalgic, as are the modern and the postmodern. The discourse of the postmodern was parasitical on the high modern insofar as it was a debate still *within* the legacy of modernism, at a critical stage: one of clarification and scepticism. Lyotard is useful in this context insofar as he argued that the postmodern condition was "undoubtedly a part of the modern", critically preparing, paradoxically, the way for a true modernity (79). It is hard to determine what "true modernity" might be exactly, but to insist that it is past is to identify the category as synonymous to the rise of Western capitalism and industrial society and its world.

In *After the End of Art*, Arthur Danto observed that, artistically, the postmodern recognised the need to go beyond the descriptor of modern, but that the postmodern was too narrow a term, designating a style we could easily recognise. Danto preferred to call the contemporary the *post-historical*, which is "a period of information disorder, a condition of perfect aesthetic entropy" (12). The philosopher admitted that it is also a "period of quite perfect freedom" without any troublesome "pale of history" (12). Understanding this transition from modernism to contemporaneity is, then, an urgent matter; it amounts to a shift from nothing less than perceived direction within history—of a modernity of point-by-point plans, avant-gardes, and systematic social programs—to a celebrated indirection, beginning in the 1970s. It is a time Danto refers to as "a period in its own way as dark as the tenth century" (12).[10] Our own contemporary modernity promotes an absence of certain historical direction-making. Our problems are not those of modernity or postmodernity; we have to face up to global warming and the long historical consequences of the biggest collective financial crisis since 1929, to name just two crises.

For Danto, contemporaneity signals a breach, or difference—not a revolutionary break, but a slide into a certain habit, attitude, and signification for the organisation of a culture that has seen the end of a particular historical narrative. The most intensified example of this can be seen in the art world today. In Danto's writing, an explicit commentary on contemporaneity emerges, with reference to the now problematised "history of art". For Danto, the condition is "post-historical", which basically means any art produced after Andy Warhol's (not revolutionary but rather terminal) *Brillo Box* (1964).

---

[10] There is, however, a positive side to this Dark Age inaugurated by Danto. The notion of "to come" was borrowed from Derrida's *The Specters of Marx* and applied to contemporary art by Smith, who insisted that "we can *not* think the art of the future in any specific, predictive sense" but we must "embrace wholeheartedly" its "unknowability as to its particulars yet inevitability as to its generality" within the contemporary condition (2001: 18). Smith writes:

… contemporaneity within art is becoming at once more complex and more central to practice. 'Contemporaneity' is an opening, constantly redefining set of forces and operations. In philosophical terms, it would be 'deconstructive' par excellence in Derrida's early sense, that has by now become at the same time an 'undeconstructible' in his more recent sense". (2001: 19)

> It is characteristic of contemporaneity—but not of modernity—that it should have begun insidiously, without slogan or logo, without anyone being greatly aware that it had happened. The Armory Show of 1913 used the pine-tree flag of the American Revolution as its logo to repudiate the art of the past. The Berlin dada movement proclaimed the death of art, but on the same poster by Raoul Hausmann wished long life to "The Machine Art of Tatlin". Contemporary art, by contrast, has no brief against the art of the past, no sense that the past is something from which liberation must be won, no sense even that it is at all different as art from modern art generally. (Danto 1997: 5)

Danto does not draw a line between the modes of production of modern and contemporary, but instead discusses the "spirit in which the art was made" (1997: 5). His argument is that "the contemporary" is defined by its relation to the art of the past and its lack of critical brief or manifesto. The art of the past is available for use in the contemporary, whereas, in the modern, the art of the past, of the classical, the Renaissance, the Romantic and Victorian, were to be variously rejected, outdone, contested, or overcome. Within the contemporary, Danto contests, the styles of the past are re-legitimated, and artists are given a freedom to do with those styles as they wish. Max Ernst's conceptually radical practice of the collage has triumphed, but, Danto points out, with a difference. For Ernst, there was a "foreign plane" upon which two distinct and different realities meet, but now, there is no longer a plane foreign enough to distinguish artistic tendencies, nor are their realities "all that distant from one another" (1997: 5). The museum as an institution has something to answer for here: "The basic perception of the contemporary spirit was formed on the principle of a museum in which all art has a rightful place, where there is no a priori criterion as to what art must look like, and where there is no narrative into which the museum's contents must all fit" (Danto 1997: 5). What we have here is not a re-heroification of art, or even a sceptical modernity, but at a third phase of modernity emptied of the precision of a positioned relationship to history, and thus the future, as such.

To describe the art that had become iconic in the public perception of "the contemporary" at the end of the century, the art critic Julian Stallabrass coined a term in the title of his book *High Art Lite*. Stallabrass argued that this art originated in Britain in the work of artists such as Damien Hirst, Jake and Dinos Chapman, Chris Ofili, and Tracey Emin, among others (the "young British artists" collected and promoted by ad mogul Charles Saatchi). The phenomenon, increasingly so, is not confined to Britain. For Stallabrass, the term captures a deceptive, press-hungry aesthetic: an "art that looks like but is not quite art, that acts as a substitute for art" (1999: 2).[11] "Since these artists", Stallabrass argues, "form an identifiable tendency that reacts against the concerns of the previous generation, they look a little like an avant-garde", which plays well for everyone, "for those liberals who want to believe that high art lite represents something radical, and for those conservatives who are afraid that it does" (1999: 4).

"Contemporaneity" cannot be used uncontested with a clear conscience; for this reason, alternatives are necessary. The use of "aftermath", offered by Smith and Foster, may be one of the stronger code-words for contemporaneity (Smith 2006b: 7), because of its heightened sense that something momentous and determining, requiring ongoing resistance to amnesia, came before. This double aftermath has considerable consequences; the passage from one concept to another concept, to take the Foucauldian stance, has not happened without certain overlappings, interactions, and echoes. Whether or not this represents, then, two "breaks" (with the postmodern as the first and contemporaneity the second) from, or corrup-

---

[11] More recently, high art lite may be conditioned by a social media-hungry aesthetic, readied for rapid "liking" and circulation on screens.

tions of, the modern remains to be seen, and remains questionable. Either way, as Foster put it, there are "other responses to this other than triumphalism or desperation, or indeed melancholy (at the very least we need not pathologise it further)" (2003: 125). Foster asks, not what comes after these ends, but "in lieu of them?" (2003: 126).

## Project or Enigma

A period without a project—a commitment to non-contemporaneous time—condemns itself to being an enigma; a portion that has no sense of the whole, too schizoid to see its own patterns, incapable of even striving to comprehend its entirety. (Consider the projected aims of the dialectic and cognitive mapping in high modern and postmodern theoretical discourse, which sought momentary illuminations of the whole). The historical paradigms of the modern and the postmodern were programmatically different from "the contemporary" of today. It is useful to draw a distinction between project and enigma to characterise how different these ontologies are. The modern and the postmodern were phenomena with structures attached to their names. The modern proposed to plan and construct, through grand designs, the collective future (and sometimes the design of a new kind of "man", such as socialist man or the Nietzschean *Übermensch* or superman); the postmodern was anti-heroic and proposed to ruthlessly deconstruct the top-down oppressions that modernity became, to resist its violent singularity. Today's contemporary, by contrast, enjoys a relatively structure-free existence. It is too ideologically broad or inclusive to have a specific object of attack or critique such as the Victorian or the Romantic, or the Modern Project itself. If modernity and postmodernity were programmatic, then contemporaneity is enigmatic in the philosopher Mario Perniola's sense of being "capable of simultaneous explanation on so many different registers of meaning, all of which are equally valid ... it is thus able to open up an intermediate space that is not necessarily bound to be filled" (1995: 10).

This indeterminate space provides a good characterisation of the experience of the long aftermath of high modern practice (which contained an escalating linear trajectory defined by identity and progress) and the immediate historical and intellectual wake of the postmodern, defined in opposition as the queering of identity and the ideology of difference. High modernity was the age of grand projects, defined by concepts of Utopia and the idea of infinite progress towards it. Postmodernity promised the deconstruction of deterministic, frequently authoritarian, modernist demands, including those of Utopia and progress, and the wholesale modernist heritage to *construct* the future through technology and scientific planning. One of the differences between the epistemes of the modern and the postmodern was the seriousness of ambition within modernity; it promised to bring about a new world, to close off once and for all feudal and Victorian darkness. It promised a clean, smooth, integrated world of international efficiency: a world market. It is an often-overlooked feature of the postmodern that it was, compared to the modern, a modest discipline. As a primary critique of the modern, postmodernity tried to put the brakes on modernity (for worldwide war, alienation, and totalitarianism had revealed its dire human consequences), but despite heralding a new era of critical sophistication, the postmodern offered no viable alternative, only difference and (eventually neo-liberal) pluralism in philosophy as much as architecture and the arts.

In *The Return of the Real*, Hal Foster noted that Western culture was swamped with "neos" and "posts" (1996: 1); he went a step further and evoked a broader "condition of coming-after" and the enigmatic "paradigm-of-no-paradigm" in his later work in *Design and Crime*, which took Thomas Kuhn's sense of the term "paradigm" to dizzying new heights (Foster 2003: 130). Foster made a case for the recursive strategy of the neo and the post in critical and theoretical discussions, which he saw as having become worn and lacking a necessarily strong oppositional status. Foster, one of the *October* art critics once committed to the construction of postmodernism as a concept (in the 1980s and early 1990s), questioned our directness of access to modernity *and* postmodernity. His argument suggests that both cultural paradigms have become historical. The periodising trilogy that advances from modernity to postmodernity to contemporaneity is schematic, but has the advantage of crystallising the problem for us. Foster states:

> ... our condition is largely one of aftermath—that we live in the wake not only of modernist painting and sculpture but of postmodernist deconstructions of these forms as well, in the wake not only of the pre-war avant-gardes but of the postwar neo-avant-gardes as well. (2003: 125)

We are, if Foster is right in his temporal assertion, in a *double* aftermath of critical thought and historical experience. There is nothing inaugural about the postmodern or "the contemporary" today.

"The contemporary" paradigm did not arrive with a grand gesture or master promise. The instituted contemporary might be better characterised as the ruin of the great twin discourses of the last century, and promises nothing—it is without program, an anti-time. Today's contemporary emerged out of global capitalism, which experienced triumph after the Cold War. That alternatives to the contemporary are rarely, if ever, offered or even considered today matches the apparent disinterest in alternatives to advanced capitalism itself (a point made numerously by Jameson and, in higher public profile, Slavoj Žižek). In high modernity, actually-existing socialism, actually-existing fascism, and actually-existing capitalism all fought for occupancy of the future. "The contemporary" is hard to challenge. It stakes out no ideology but it does have one: that of striving for invisibility. It has the advantage of feeling relatively free of negative association. At worst, it is lacking. Groys called it hesitant, broad, horizonless, and structure-free. It holds a strong connection to global capitalism as a category, although there is (unlike within the cultural ontology of the modern) no triumphal arrival, no sense of relief, no respite after the century of nuclear devastation, planned megadeath, and planned techno-obsolescence; it exists without a project, which effectively means no future as such. (We are in an age, to borrow a nineteenth century metaphor, which builds engines on railroads without destinations.)

Unlike modernity, this is not an age of projects in terms of the kind sought by the Modern Movement in architecture, or even Stalinist plans (which are of the same modality, namely of the detailed collective road toward an achievable Utopia). In contemporary times, we are not on the road toward anything except perhaps environmental or financial collapse; more of the likes of Hurricane Katrina or tsunamis in the Indian Ocean or some other potential catastrophe or generalised bust or decline: the end of resources, or an all-out war for their monopoly (witness the arrogant and aggressive role of North America in the Middle East and elsewhere). It is arguable that the new periodising hypothesis, which includes environmental meltdown and global power shifts (such as indicated by the rise of China), functions to give us critical distance on old theoretical paradigms so that we can begin to map the constitutive features of successive developments. (An effort to stake out the institutional aesthetics and architectures of these developments is to be found in the next two chapters of this book.) Scientific projects such as the Millennium Seed Bank and efforts to reverse extinction of plants and animals (de-extinction) do constitute commitment to non-contemporaneous time; however, they are dystopian by design, readying for the worst possible scenarios after the end of Nature as such.

It will be instructive to apply Jameson's maxim that "Modernity is not a concept but a narrative category" (2002: 94) to "the contemporary". The term might then be less practically grasped as a concept than as a site awaiting narrative construction. Within postmodernity, which developed between 1945 and 1989 (but intensified between the 1960s and the 1980s), the Cold War defined a contest between socialism and capitalism, with capitalism always ascendant. The culture of contemporary modernity or contemporaneity belongs to the long sought-after triumph of capitalism. Postmodernity needs to be understood as a discourse that arrived out of, and in order to explain, the Cold War, predicated on the implication—with the hydrogen bomb—of the hottest war imaginable. The American war in Vietnam and the many attempts to rethink culture by the generation of 1968, as well as the Reagan-Thatcher era in the 1980s and the end of Soviet-style socialism itself, cannot be added up to equal a satisfactory answer to the question of postmodern times, but, as a constellation, provides a limit to the concept of the postmodern as a narrative category. The use of the term postmodern to designate the Cold War state of paranoid political-international affairs dominated by an image of two superpowers competing against each other (yet really doing the same kind of thing, for the prestige of the moon landing, accumulation of high-tech weapons, etc.) represents something of a generational limit. In this sense, contemporaneity names the "project" of late capitalist growth (spatially, not temporally or committed to the non-contemporaneous future) connected to globalisation that succeeded the end of the Soviets that constituted a massive dilation of the late capitalist sphere.

The debate about a "paradigm shift" (Kuhn again) from postmodernism to globalisation is an interesting one in this context. Globalisation (whether positively or negatively imagined), too, seems antiquated, rich in association with the Bill Clinton and Junichiro Koizumi era, and the Paul Keating era in Australia. Contemporaneity might be grasped, after having such thoughts, as the partial, yet significant, product of globalisation that we are *left with* even after the globalisation era has not so much finished, as "collapsed" (collapse being the basic organisational insight, in economic thought, of the Canadian thinker John Ralston Saul's *The Collapse of Globalism*). The collapse of globalism rests on the insistence of globalism's relative success (i.e. globalism must succeed in order to fail), as Saul rightly registers, and as expansive economic, political, and technological realities, as well as an ideology in the form of a belief in the inevitability of the globalising narrative, of its synonymousness with progress, and of North America's historical hegemony (Saul 2005: 111). Certainly, among the many subtle components of Saul's reading, one of the central features lies in his remarking on the return of aggressive nationalism in the example of the US and coalition-led military invasions of the last decade. War always produces nationalism, or vice versa. According to Saul, the waning of the nation-state was hailed in the 1990s by globalists as the sure sign that the global and world market system was triumphing over earlier, inferior times, ideologies, and states.[12]

"The contemporary" and its logic of dissemination throughout museums belongs to the narrative of globalisation. The contemporary is, therefore, the name for a crisis in the museumification of culture, not its resolution. As cities and regions link up through the great multifaceted process of globalisation, they enter into contemporaneity with each oth-

---

[12] The opposite line of thinking about the strong continuation of the nation-state is exhibited in the economist Thomas L. Friedman's *The World is Flat: A Brief History of the Twenty-first Century*. Friedman's worldview and argument, unlike that of Saul's, operates on the other end of the political spectrum and is pro-American in its *raison d'être* of preserving US hegemony over India and China in today's "flat" world; since Columbus' accidental journey to America in the fifteenth century we have been accustomed to thinking of it as "round". Friedman, to simplify, speaks of the world as flat in the sense that the playing field of the world market system has been levelled out by the forces of globalisation, which includes everything from the fall of communism at the end of the 1980s to the rise of the Internet and the laying down of vast fibre-optic cables, the open sourcing of today's online software (an increasingly derailed project), and the outsourcing of labour markets. The contemporary might be considered, within this picture as the aesthetic opposite of the modern, which was not flat but irregular or downright jagged in its occupation of a future space of which the colonies, the "primitive" peoples, and the Third World could only dream. However, Friedman's own position would drag the contemporary back into a jagged, near pre-contemporary state in which the US rules top down.

er and seal (or monumentalise) the deal in the cultural act of opening a new museum devoted to the empty and essentially contentless term that serves to positively diagnose the new spatial connection and shared—or at least simultaneous—experience of expanded space and economic potential (both for profit and collapse). Globalisation shifts the gears of local time consciousness and spatial awareness as it lifts the contemporary out of the non-contemporary. More people are uploaded onto the same temporal plane than at any point in history, and "the contemporary" becomes, for lack of anything more explanatory or exemplary, the word that apprehends the process. This is not a project as such but a moment of massive, logical expansion of the system into the great new economic and social space opened up by commodification.

## Art in "the contemporary"

The preconditions—technological, transportational, political, economic, social, etc. (but not necessarily in that order)—were such that the discursive explosion of contemporaneity was "global", with all of the structures of prejudice in the guise of inclusiveness that that term indicates today. A lot of art and artefacts circulate within the networks (biennale, art fair, travelling or mobile exhibitions) of "the contemporary", but that is really all they do; that they merely circulate and accrue status threatens to empty the works of their critique. A critical attitude is nominally present, but is a world away from the programmatic notions witnessed by high modernity and, especially, postmodernity. Undoubtedly, the commodity fetishism of Theodor Adorno or Marx (albeit a high culture variant), promoted by the market, is responsible. Here, serious consequences come into view. If the institutions of art and culture (like the university system), once harbingers of critical and aesthetic autonomy, cannot assert positive definitions or articulate a direction for contemporaneity—however against the grain that may be—other more authoritarian figures and forces will not hesitate to step forward in order to define and occupy, to add their own content (economic rationalism, the authoritarianism of the market war, nationalism) to the open signifier which we call "the contemporary".

The contemporary emerges without a strong engagement with the forces that helped to bring it into being—that is, without a story binding back to modernity and postmodernity. High modernity was bound by a belief in the future—an immanent future that would be brought about through technology. The city, the building, and the human, became a system of interlocking efficient machines in Le Corbusier's modernist Utopianism. Postmodernity queried and "ended" the modern project in as many ways as it could muster; debates occurred on the *end* of all kinds of things, from art and ideology to history and theory, and even to the category of "man" itself in Foucault's *The Order of Things.* Yet, the postmodern was still parasitical on the modern. A positive future was implied by the postmodern, for all its nihilism, through the very act of negating or challenging the now-terrifying consequences of modernity, named especially by Zygmunt Bauman in *Modernity and the Holocaust.*

The institutional use of the word contemporary has knocked many possible alternatives out of circulation and, in turn, has launched itself into the position of common sense. Especially in the continued high culture of art and museums it has developed a privileged status: the status of commodity fetish in the classical Marxian sense of the term. It has been instituted with extraordinary deliberation, not by chance. Once registered and made official by the establishment, the term became habitual for the art press, the publishing houses, the art markets, and the museum-going public, and was used instinctively; the contemporary becomes an automatic, albeit empty, critique.

The contemporary paradigm arguably emerged in the 1980s (the canonisation of Warhol, Pop Art, Found Art, Outsider Art, etc.) at a critical moment in which the Modern had become suspect and the postmodern remained too alienating for the non-academic establishment (it was also alienating within academia, and indeed that was a part of its project: to blow apart academic conventions). The contemporary also oversaw the launching of commodification as an end in itself (as a career choice for artists, though not for the many), extending as a model of practice from Warhol to Jeff Koons and Takashi Murakami, blurring the traditional, pre-contemporary lines between art and mass product. Its full institutionalisation took place in the 1990s when the term was conspicuously rendered on museum and gallery entrances, and when alternative art spaces used it as a framing device for their critical endeavours. The term, then, offered a safe option between the two troublemakers (modern and postmodern), awaiting construction.

In art, "the contemporary" is a temporal descriptor, but it is also, as the Wyndham Lewis epigraph above indicates, an evaluative measure taken against cultural phenomena. As an evaluative measure, the contemporary designates an opposite number, namely of non-contemporary artistic practices, technologies, persons, and artefacts (non-élite and powerless ones). For a work to be admitted into the contemporary it must conform to a defined, if broad, set of expectations that amount to an attitude or relation to artistic objecthood. The word presents an inclusive category, but it is as much the mark of an exclusive territorialisation that has its root in the anti-aesthetic, anti-display, and anti-museum apparatus that was Marcel Duchamp's *Fountain* of 1917—that great readymade, topsy-turvy urinal that at once invented a wholly new conception of art as object, and the artist as curator of objects and displacer of established paradigms. Duchamp's reading of the future of art was that artists would one day not make things but simply point at them and declare them art; in this he pre-empted the *post-expressionist* paradigms of art today. The traceable rise of "contemporary art", institutionally and globally, was an act of definition and major ideological construction the likes of which had only been seen in the rise of Modern Art in the last century, and the Modern Movement in architecture (which had the authority to define and generate desire beyond their disciplines). Modern Art underwent an enormous amount of construction, institutionally, before it became consensual, whether as something to be celebrated or derided. It was argued for in non-institutional exhibitions and manifestoes. It was hated and rejected until its eventual love and acceptance.[13]

Not all art that is contemporary is "contemporary art", which is discursively more regimented than its aura of creative freedom would imply.[14] In the development of contemporary art, the Modern Project (or modernity) was not present to support such a construction. The contemporary, theoretically, can be made up of anything because it has nowhere to go, no *telos*, no path to Being or Spirit; however, in practice, this is not the case. The phenomenon Adorno and Horkheimer called the "consciousness industries" (1979) retains some determining control over levels of aesthetic acceptability: what is and what is not to be classified as contemporary art, who is and who is not allowed to name it as such. Capital plays a key role here. Artworks have to be constructed, not created, just as artists themselves are constructed, and very often circulated, in the realms of representation, so that they accrue social and cultural capital, so that they have *meaning* in the superficial market sense of objective monetary value. Museums are crucial in this respect, and so is the work of historians and critics.

The wide institutional avoidance of the terms today—modern (with few exceptions), and postmodern (no one has successfully founded a Museum of Postmodern Art, and, as

---

[13] Consider the story of American abstract expressionism, in which case modern art appears to have been rejected until the right national powers were behind it, at least in the US.

[14] For a very good discussion of how art and capitalist value are constructed via hollow networks of branding, see Don Thompson's *The $12 Million Stuffed Shark: The Curious Economics of Art and Auction Houses*. See also Julian Stallabrass' *Art Incorporated: The Story of Contemporary Art*. Stallabrass has developed an unstated Marxist critique of the current global art world culture that tries to show how that which we think is most free in our culture is in fact a zone of regulation and incorporation into the established system.

many have already pointed out, it is arguably too late now)—indicates a preference for that which is less constructed, less dogmatic, less rigid with programmatic assertion and association. The contemporary becomes a kind of apology for Perniola's enigma: a pseudo-object, a non-category to fill the void. It does not represent a desire for change or a trajectory into the future. The contemporary of "contemporary art" is in general more political than historical modernist art (with its comparatively less direct politics of autonomy and abstraction), yet it lacks the surrounding critical discourse, or metanarrative, of onward progress towards a new world that deposits the degraded present of our own experience into the "dustbin of history" (as Leon Trotsky famously put it). The contemporary is embedded in the perpetual free-market present that is the closest thing we have to a collective, objective reality in the early twenty-first century. The contemporary may be the end to which the architect Sze Tsung Leong, parodic apologist for global capitalism, referred when he wrote that "in the end, there will be little else for us to do but shop" (cited in Jameson 2003: 77).

What is extraordinary to observe in this context is the way that the future is reduced to the present—the world of tomorrow is conceived as being an unbroken continuation of the present (i.e., with the culture of consumption and satisfaction found in images at its centre). Through something like the US debt, it is important for capitalism to be the "end of history" or a continuous present, as a change of system would challenge the whole economy of the debt. Jürgen Habermas' insistence on the "incompletion" of modernity is a useful critique and should be remembered in self-satisfied situations like that of Leong's; the conception of an ontological lack in Habermas' argument had the virtue of giving everyone something to do. A similar insistence on the contemporary as a transitional phase, rather than an endpoint, eternal historyless plateau, or achieved (albeit fake) Utopia also gives us something to do. The postmodern loss of metanarratives is to be bemoaned here, as they function to activate the historical imagination (myth and enchantment still have much work to do)—to patch the isolated, fetishised "contemporary" back into dialogue with the past, a precondition for making a sense of the future as an alternative to the present appear.

## Paradoxical Globalism

"The contemporary", or modernity without a project, indicates the arrival of a state that goes beyond the already constructed (but never finalized) articulations of the epochs of the modern and the postmodern. It also marks a shift in their corresponding material bases of multinational, or late, capitalism. Multinational capitalism (used interchangeably here with global capitalism) continues in the aftermath of the discourses of the high modern and the sceptical postmodern, but its territories are changing, perhaps fundamentally. The changes that have occurred since Ernest Mandel published his classic *Late Capitalism* in 1972; used by Jameson to theorise the cultural logic of postmodernity, it was limited as an account to the long post-war international economic boom, which is surely not ours. The term post-late capitalism can perhaps be applied here. Indeed, it is the task of artists, critics, and scholars of contemporaneity as a critical, complex stance towards the high tech (yet fragile) global present to offer some grid coordinates—most of which will be architectural-financial—of the cultural logic that comes after Jameson and Mandel. "The postmodern", in its critical currency, was a push to unify debate across spheres and disciplines usually closed to each other, even if in fact it primarily resulted in further antagonism and polarisation.

While Mandellian or Jamesonian "late capitalism" is obviously the force enacting historical amnesia and generalised socialist shutdown (or systemic alternatives of any kind to "fellow travel" with)—although crucial contradictions to its state of affairs have arisen and continue in Latin America, particularly Venezuela and Bolivia, for instance—the "contemporary" cultural conjuncture, if not equal to a paradigmatic shift altogether, does indicate change (not necessarily for the better). The critically astute artists and architects of "the contemporary" paradigm are trying in diverse ways to generate a new sense or negotiation with these conditions in their work. As Terry Smith argued in "World Picturing in Contemporary Art", contemporaneity is therefore a kind of "world picturing" concept in Martin Heidegger's sense, but this time for an age that throws the very notion of a coherent world picture itself into question.

"Contemporaneity" is not equal to historical modernity or postmodernity. It is instructive to use Smith's account of contemporary modernity, which he conceives under the somewhat passive rubric of "changing time" that will bring forth a startling mosaic of events and processes. It is worthwhile quoting Smith extensively on this matter to glimpse into the elements of a situation of situations, made up of alienated collective events. Smith sees this situation as indicating a combination of "profound realignments between the great formations of modernity" (2008: 2) and also what appears to be the "emergence of what may be new formations" (2008: 2):

> The 9/11 moment is a recent flashpoint of both civilizational and region-to-region conflict, and it continues to be used as a justification for governments of all stripes to declare open-ended states of emergency, and as an umbrella for the imposition of repressive agendas in many countries, not least the United States. Intractable, irresolvable "events" of this kind have come to seem almost normal in the state of aftermath: the wars in Afghanistan and Iraq; the uncertain prospect of a US imperium; the question of European polity, internally and externally; the implosive fallout of the Second World and the reemergence of authoritarianism and "democracy" within it; in the ex-Soviet peripheries, the suddenness of unReal states, and of the apparent extension of Europe; continuing conflicts in the Middle East, Central Europe, Africa, and the Pacific; the deadly inadequacy of tribalism versus modernization as models for decolonisation in Africa; the crisis of post-WWII international institutions (UN, IMF, World Bank);

the revival of leftist governments in South America; the accelerating concentration of wealth in few countries, and within those countries its concentration in the few; ecological time bombs everywhere, and the looming threat of societal collapse; the ubiquity and diversification of specular culture; the concentration and narrowing of media versus the spread of internet; contradictions within and between regulated and coercive economies and cultures within singular state formations (most prominently, now, China); the proliferation of protest movements and alternative networks; the retreat towards bunker architecture and proliferation of ingenious, adaptive architecture in the borderzones of swelling cosmopoli; and the emergence of distinctively different models of appropriate artistic practice, as manifested in major survey exhibitions, such as *Documenta II* of 2002 and the 50th Venice Biennale in 2003, along with the retreat into compromise that has marked curatorial planning since—with some exceptions, such as the 2006 *Sydney Biennale*. (2008: 2–3)

These manifestations, as Smith notes, are only some of the most visible "formations and fissures" registered at the most public, political levels. Many of these elements seem familiar from accounts of modernity and postmodernity, yet, as Smith goes on to suggest, "something about the mix, the mood and the outcome seems to be becoming more and more distinctive" (2008: 3). What we can immediately deduce about contemporary modernity is that no one in the world is adequately positioned to give a detailed account of the phenomenon in all of its aspects. The fragmentation of societies—part of the postmodern condition as well—obviously continues deep enough into "the contemporary", while giving an account of the totality was hardly conceived as a problem for high modernists whose belief dictated that progress and the culture of the modern or enlightenment simply had to be exported to the rest of humanity; paradoxically, it is the global society whose experience is fundamentally fragmented. The necessary response is to reveal the unevenness, the staggered nature of such phenomena, and to insist on the relative incompleteness of the picture and the inevitability of further events being produced by these events—new situations produced by these situations—as they barge up against each other in the post-Cold War, post-9/11, and, now, post-money crash world. It may be most encompassing to refer to this as a *situation of situations*, as a network of concepts and historic nodes more than a single concept or event. One could keep adding to such a list (the Arab Spring, numerous natural disasters, a nascent commercial space tourist race), yet this still would not necessarily bring us closer to an understanding of its components or a give us relief from the sense of numbness such a compilation tends to sponsor. What are needed are micro cognitive maps that show how the experience of individual parts of this picture is in fact legible and interesting in a tangible, broader theoretical scheme. A new kind of experiential literacy in terms of paradoxical globalism is needed this century; one could do worse than look for a model in the archive of diverse dialectical materialisms.

In a final deployment of "contemporaneity" as a structure for epochal thought, we can turn to Ernst Bloch and the global historian Wolf Schafer's use of the term. Bloch's theory in Schafer's interpretation refers to a "historico-philosophical theory" (Schafer 2004: 116). Schafer, in turn, has attempted to construct contemporaneity as a concept that embodies the "asynchronous simultaneity" of cultures within global modern history—a state that is changing within contemporaneity—deployed as a periodising hypothesis. Contemporaneity to him is a positive attempt to overcome the temporal arrogance of modernity, with its tendency to imagine a modernity for everyone, even if, or especially if, that means by force (look at the many-tentacled history of European colonialism). In a stark and original image, Schafer views the current age as having begun to achieve a techno-scientific "Pangaea Two", a "consciously shared global environment", in which the globe has drifted towards a defragmenting of old structures and nation-states with the development of global networks (109).

Schafer does seem overly celebratory in the way theorists of globalisation have often been, focused more on the ecstasy of such a situation rather than its consequences. "The temporal focus", he declares, "of global history is neither the past, as in mythomaniac times, nor the future, as in modern times, but the present contemporaneity of all humans" (109). This, however, leads Schafer to his arguably ominous critique of "the ideology of non-contemporaneity", in which "not all contemporaries are contemporaneous" (109).

I do not recommend trying to say what the contemporary *is*. At any rate, there are plenty of museums and other institutions in the process of doing that, both high and low. The method of the Nietzschean genealogy has much to recommend it and provides an alternative to writing a "history" of contemporaneity, aiming to proclaim some eventual objective truth.

We can, however, make some positive statements without succumbing to the metaphysical.

#1. The term "contemporaneity" is a critical term that has emerged as a fitting, yet uneven substitute for the once powerful critiques of modernity and postmodernity; its users want to return a sense of history and a picture of wider scope to the vapid uses of "the contemporary". Its appearance registers the double waning of their complex responses to the great civilisational crises (within the last two hundred years at least) of rapid industrialisation, the rise of the metropolis, the alienation of the subject, the emergence of high-tech global conflict, competing global ideologies, and globalisation itself, among a multiplicity of other emergencies and events. Contemporaneity is an attempt to grasp the unique cultural condition that succeeds—but not in a triumphal way—the aftermath of modernity and the more recent consensual break away from the critical discourse of the postmodern. In short, my survey of the term has tried to register a paradox indicated by the philosopher Mario Perniola, to recognise an *enigma that does not have to be solved*.

#2. If modernity sought universalisation through technology and culture, the contemporary institutes the deep-freeze preservation of differences. If modernity and postmodernity have been revealed as European or North American-centric phenomena, that is in terms of a soft (and occasionally hard) cultural imperialism, "the contemporary" provisionally suspends the older terms and offers a non-space—a stasis from which to operate. The contemporary can be said to have one grand promise: that is, in Schafer's terms, to "upload all of humanity onto the same temporal plane" (119). It is a basic condition of post-globalisation; the contemporary promises access to the present for everyone in the form of the democratisation of a once élite modality. The dissemination of Museums of Contemporary Art in our time reflects this cultural preference, this implied right, this severe, permanent but ever-changing, zero degree.

#3. We construct, rather than discover, our contemporaneity. If contemporaneity is a global state that current societies aspire to, it is, like Kant argued of the Enlightenment, *not yet achieved*. Contemporaneity is not, however, Utopian. Rather, it nascently exists, not as the horrifyingly homogenous space that anti-globalists feared but as the cultural illusion of difference for everyone. The world market is the avenue which the democratisation of temporality is currently taking. I have argued that contemporaneity is emergent, and that we (via Kant) may not be in fully blown contemporaneity, but in an *age of contemporaneity*. It is, then, to be understood as a bumpy new territory.

4. At the centre of "the contemporary" is a breathless concentration on human creativity and the processes of self-invention in the face of nothing. Yet, contemporaneity is not a crisis. It does not demand to be solved. It is, at any rate, not cohesive enough to be solved. The contemporary, in the museums, is close to the functions of the market, following season change and fashion rather than outlining its own trajectory; this is problematic. It is what Jameson would have called,

in the 1980s, "schizophrenic", meaning that the links in a signifying chain have been broken. The contemporary is an instituted enigma. It has no project and no direction. It has still not really clearly stated its purpose; the contemporary has had no manifesto. As my reading of Danto has hopefully suggested, it is the space for an ever-changing image, from any time.

#5. Nowhere is the deployment of a purposeless "contemporary" more evident than in the museums and galleries of today's cultural institutions. As businesses, the museums, the galleries, and also the publishing houses that package their identities—all implicated in the construction of the contemporary—are part of the mode of production and the short term artificiality of the commercialised seasons. What we end up with then, as Rem Koolhaas morbidly observed of his own career as a subject of the global capitalist system in architecture, is a "random sequence of commissions" and "the opposite of an agenda" (2004a: 20). In other words, as lifeless, dissociated, and manufactured events. The essential point to grasp is that contemporaneity still stands as a critique without commitment—a kind of empty, yet perpetual gesture towards an exit from that which we presently perceive as reality. In this lies an explanation for Koolhaas' dual identity as architect and writer. Koolhaas' parallel project of writing stories around architectural units—his own and those of earlier and other architects—is an attempt to return narrative to the experience and trajectory of internal fragmentation in contemporary modernity. Scripting becomes both apologetics for capitalist mutations and a radical experiment in meaning (but more on Koolhaas in chapter four).

#6. A positive reading of "the contemporary" and contemporaneity might allow us some renewed freedom, and ground of possibilities, reconnection and construction. This has been offered here (in the margins, as it were), using the idea of the enigma. In all of these attempts to think of the contemporary, we are faced with the unavoidably paradoxical: trying to recognise a condition that succeeds the twin megalithic codes of the modern and the postmodern, while unavoidably cannibalising those terms in the very act of reading into each dispensation of the contemporary. This, I argue, is not something to be overcome, but a tension that pursues us the whole way of the journey. In contemporaneity lies a contradiction that is not to be resolved; unlike modernity, which sought to resolve through the dialectic, and unlike postmodernity, which argued for a difference against the totalitarian grand narratives of modernity, what we are seeing in the enigma is the repetition of a category that has all the outward signs of modernity—a commitment to now—but none of modernity's future orientation, none of its substance, none of its once essential *program*. It is incessantly, obsessively present-oriented because it has nowhere to go, no future except more of itself.

#7. In all of this there is a tacit acceptance of the global in "the contemporary". This has not always been the case. It is indicative of the age of history through which we are passing. It is not unusual to travel from New York to Tokyo or Sydney to Helsinki (or virtually wherever) and find what seems to be near-identical installations of art in a state gallery or museum, or even in privately owned galleries (such as the Saatchi Gallery or Tasmania's Museum of Old and New Art [MONA]) with apparently little more than what Adorno called "pseudo-differentiation" between installations: the same artists' names, often works from the same series, often the same architect-designed style of building, and an identical approach to display. It all has a common vogue of plurality and a heightened awareness of the idea that painting and sculpture are not the whole story of twentieth-century art. True enough. The cities themselves remain distinct, with different histories of tradition and traditions of history, and iconic deployments of architecture. A kind of curatorial agreement that is virtually unspoken and unexplored runs between them in the contemporary, like a shared hallucination of being in time at the same time, divided spatially (and often socially and economically), but simultaneous in their temporalities.

#8. Nietzschean-Foucauldian genealogy *is* a theory of contemporaneity. When Foucault developed his arguments on modernity in the essays "Nietzsche, Genealogy, History" and "What is Enlightenment?" it was evidently contemporaneity that he sought an approach to reveal all along. His intention was to open up a framework for reading the products of culture and philosophy in a way that would enable new contents to contradict the sterilities of a present overlaid or explained, all too readily, with official or orthodox narratives about the past and who we are. This is of course to read Foucault outside of his own terms, to interpret his thinking for our own use. We should do this, it might be added, but not with the anxiety of getting the philosopher wrong—he is notorious for having been misinterpreted and misappropriated. It should be done in the style of pronouncing a foreign name for the first time: loudly and with confidence. Following Foucault, genealogy continues to provide a usefulness in the way that it "disturbs what was previously considered immobile", "fragments what was thought unified" and "shows the heterogeneity of what was imagined consistent with itself" (1991: 82).

#9. Finally, one thinks of the 1960s' call to *name* the system—to locate a collective site of meaning to struggle against. By this token, discussion of "the contemporary" (in particular, its extraordinary proliferation and rise as an institutional force), must have a deep connection to the maintenance of the system, global capitalism, and the obvious ills of its excesses as a "society of the spectacle", as Guy Debord and the Situationists called it. Every theory of the contemporary must confront its existence. Or perhaps, on the contrary, it is not deployed as maintenance at all but is merely ideological fallout of a system that is teetering on the edge of a risky existence: a terminal identity, hyper-aware of its presence in the here and now, like one of Franz Kafka's paranoid subjects—always languishing in the perceived danger of the present. My analysis of this phenomenon, then, has proceeded by arcing into the past, up to Kant and down to Foucault and the MCAs. The contemporary must somehow come to terms with the fact that its future is always more contemporaneity. In the next chapter, the Museum of Modern Art is read as a site where the unavoidability of the category and experience of "the contemporary" today is negotiated.

## 03: Remaking the Museum of Modern Art

> The word "modern" is valuable because semantically it suggests the progressive, original and challenging rather than the safe and academic which would naturally be included in the supine neutrality of the term "contemporary".
> Alfred H. Barr, Jr.

The New York Museum of Modern Art (MoMA) has had the great collective project of modernity—the whole complex process behind modernism—as the core of its business. Early in the 2000s, MoMA underwent massive expansion. The museum's architect Yoshio Taniguchi used the occasion of reconstruction to redeploy minimalist architecture in a formal language of parallel lines, large rectangular planes, and a continued rejection of ornament (excluding the art, a kind of "ornament" in its own right, that the museum is designed to exhibit). While minimalism was the museum's established aesthetic mode, it was not obliged to reuse the style at this time. Here, I argue that the "new" museum perpetuated Alfred H. Barr, Jr's founding curatorial notion of MoMA understood not as a mausoleum (the critique of museums laid down by the Italian Futurists) but as a laboratory of experiment and effects, even as this was apparently cancelled by the non-experimental form of the new building. What we have here is not a postmodern critique of the modern but an extension of the original revolutions of modernity in its most élite, conspicuously commoditised version.

It makes sense to revisit the history of MoMA at this time, as yet more expansion projects are being announced that will define the next era for the museum (monsters and financial crashes notwithstanding)—that is, until the next expansion or redefinition, and so on. The constancy of announcements of expansions underscores the ethos below the microscope in this chapter. In modernity, art became provisional; more recently, architecture has followed suit.

MoMA's original "object" was not an object as such, but a process, an attitude, a practice: the modern, which MoMA sought to define from the inside. The museum's institutionalisation of "the contemporary"—an innovation unique to the latest reconstruction—points to the museum's entry into a changed world. Why did the museum seek to redefine itself as contemporary at this time? Why had it not redefined itself in this way earlier? Why was this museum in particular so late to arrive? The answers to these questions are complex and require an extended examination of MoMA's history up to the point of reconstruction, which was in process by the end of the millennium although it did not reopen its doors to the public until 2004 (meanwhile it relocated to a temporary headquarters in an old single-storey staple factory in Queens, arguably more in the vogue of "contemporary" than its Manhattan headquarters). There are multiple angles from which to look at the reconstruction—directorial, architectural, art-historical, curatorial—all of which are pressurised in various ways by the discourse of "the contemporary", which had forged an unshakable place for itself in the artistic, intellectual, and public imaginations.

If we judge the reconstruction by how the collection is mobilised, we find in its deployment of the contemporary a zone without structure and direction, something that Hal Foster, writing in the *London Review of Books*, recognised, "the Contemporary Galleries come across as a prehistorical holding pen, a space without a story" (2004: 25). If we judge the reconstruction by the architecture, we find an undeconstructed modernist, minimalist rendering, marked by two absences: the irony of postmodernist architecture and the spectacle of *shape* that has become virtually hegemonic in museum practice since Frank Gehry's Guggenheim Museum in Bilbao, Spain. The reasons for these absences are various. The reconstructed MoMA reveals a modernism without a project, an empty or hollowed out modernism, the motions of modernism without its ethic of the future. For MoMA, as for the contemporary and the enigma, the future is imagined as a repetition of what already exists. In this sense, it is not strictly *a future* at all. The discourse of the contemporary acknowledges that there is no way to prepare for *the future* after all. MoMA has been reshaped to deal with the new realities of a directionless global capitalism that functions without a plan, and indeed thrives on its rudderlessness. In this context, MoMA provides no ground rules. Its use of "the contemporary" indicates an empty openness to that which might arrive from any direction and consist of almost any material or shape.

## Torpedo to Enigma

Museum space is an almost readymade category in which to build an argument about contemporaneity. The cultural site of the museum emerged in its modern form at the time of the French Revolution and the radical transformation of the Louvre. It has been understood as focused firmly on the past, as a storage and retrieval system for collective consciousness. Yet, museums have entertained a secret relation to their own present—in other words, another function. They developed within modernity, as Andreas Huyssen argued in *Twilight Memories*, into cultural constructions in the present designed to compensate for the losses of tradition perpetually experienced in rapidly modernising and increasingly future-oriented societies; the "dead eye of the storm of progress serving as catalyst for the articulation of tradition and nation, heritage and canon" (Huyssen: 13). Modern societies do not have free or neutral interests in their own pasts. The Louvre, for instance, was a showcase for bourgeois revolution, as a monument to the temporal disruption of the vast feudal regimes of Europe. The museum, while a site of power and hegemony per se, did not conspicuously seek to construct and act as a guiding force for modern societies. Then, the traditional museum, even as a "state apparatus" in the Marxist sense, was passive. It settled for *reflection*; it did not have its own agenda, its own program.

MoMA introduced a key differentiation and innovation from museums of the past in this regard. MoMA had a strong sense of the heroic present that Baudelaire, and later Ezra Pound, championed. The institution presented itself (especially when its purpose-built, Bauhaus-inspired building was developed in 1939) with a clear linear vision of its place in time as an agent of change within the present. MoMA, unlike the museums of contemporary art today, had a central philosophy. The founding of MoMA in 1929 was therefore partly a reflection of the European avant-garde vision and crucially, because of Alfred H. Barr, Jr's critical vision, partly *an extension* of that avant-garde culture. MoMA was part of the whole critical arsenal of modern culture. This is the museum's twentieth century legacy. In the twenty-first, we are witnesses of another emergence: a reminting of the modern in the discourse of "the contemporary". The revival of minimalist architecture offers a seemingly neutral formalism. In art itself, we see an obsessive and official urge to show the present moment, the cult of the "genius" artist, and unpleasant insistences on meaning. All this is occurring, however, without modernism's historical commitment to a future envisioned as being different to our own present.

The strongest theoretical statements of historical modernist aesthetic teleology were formulated at the Museum of Modern Art. It introduced a radical new self-image of the cultural institution of the museum. Barr's metaphor from the late 1920s, which he used to describe the rise and trajectory of modern art, was a torpedo moving through time (Fig. 2). The torpedo is an élite and powerful modernist icon, a celebration of technology and speed. Above all, the torpedo portrays programmability and direction, even when aimed at disintegration; modernism has long used the idea of destruction as a *creative* act.

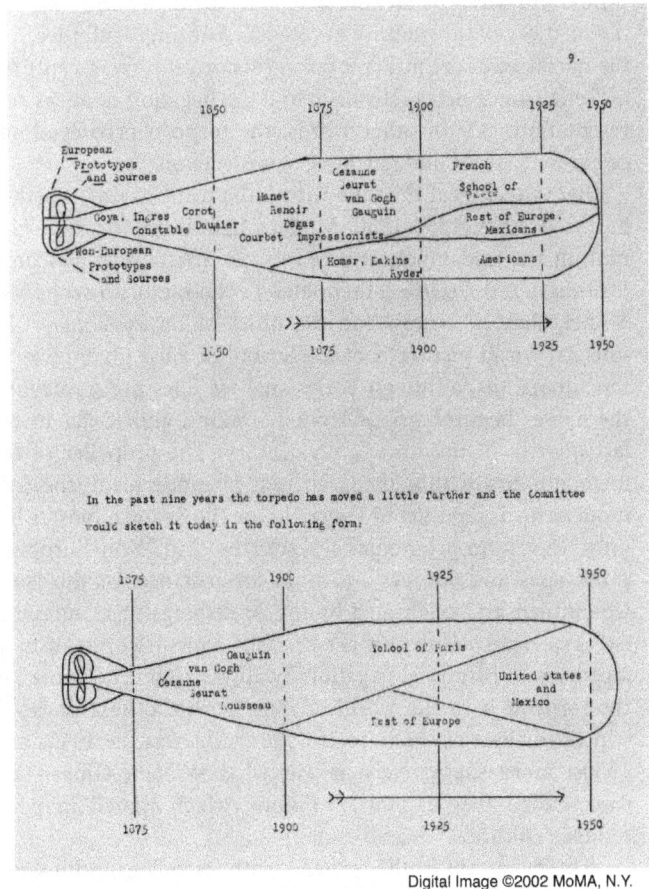

*Figure 2.* Alfred Hamilton Barr, Jr., 'Torpedo' diagrams of the ideal permanent collection of The Museum of Modern Art, as advanced in 1933 (top) and in 1941 (bottom), 1941. © 2014. Digital image, The Museum of Modern Art, New York/Scala, Florence.

Barr's theoretical vision for the museum was unlike any before. It was straight out of the European avant-garde with which he had become increasingly and personally acquainted; the museum *was* a manifesto. In the torpedo lay a temporal vision. MoMA, for all its openness to the new technologies (film) and styles (machine aesthetic, Bauhaus and *international style*), was primarily devoted to painting, sculpture, and the narrative of the militant break (historically, from centuries of Renaissance perspectivalism and the negation of art as representation). Or in other words, the torpedo privileged and celebrated the art and narrative of abstraction.

Barr's technical timeline within the torpedo was exactly a hundred years: 1850-1950. Modern painting finds its beginning in the mid-nineteenth century in artists such as Corot, Daumier, and Courbet, then later in the rapid succession of Manet, Renoir, Degas, and the onset of impressionism. Its internal world picture is of the School of Paris giving way to the Americans, although Barr's analysis does not go beyond the naïve "beginnings" of Homer, Dakins, and Ryder in the last quarter of the nineteenth century. The propeller of the metaphor lies within the deep past of modernism; the first modern art is credited to Goya. Before the Spanish master lies only "European prototypes and sources" and "Non-European prototypes and sources". (Think, for instance, of the "pre-Colombian art" celebrated by the Arensbergs in a "modernist" American context.) It is essentially a picture of Realism in a process of historical negation by abstraction. The "nose" of the torpedo is in the world of tomorrow, the next phase of which, for Barr at the time of its drawing, was the 1940s and 1950s; more suggestively, it was what William Gibson has since called the "capital F" Future, which waned in postmodern culture.

The metaphor of the torpedo, with its violent technology, speed, and capacity to destroy that which exists, lies in a tradition of militaristic imagery for modern art. This is evident in the notion of the "avant-garde" itself: a concept borrowed from the front-line of war. Barr wrote: "its nose the ever advancing present, its tail the ever receding past of fifty to a hundred years ago" (Kantor: 366). The torpedo remains necessary to explain the "modern" mission of MoMA. The torpedo is useful today for demonstrating the lack of an ideology of, a belief in, and direction at MoMA today, which is hesitant. The contemporary has no equivalent metaphor of absolute direction.

In the late 1990s, MoMA made the decision to reconstruct itself—to *contemporise*. Between 2000 and 2004 it carried out massive reconstruction according to the redesign of the museum's entire campus by Taniguchi.[1] It was mostly a building site when the Manhattan World Trade Center was attacked in September, 2001. MoMA conceived of its reconstruction around the binary of the terms *modern* and *contemporary*. All the consequential decisions were made at the high point of globalism and the "economic prism", and thus became the most extensive rebuilding, renovation, and reminting project in its history. Globalism, following John Ralston Saul, is at the centre of the disconnection between the modern, which was always international but not exclusively market-driven, and "the contemporary".

---

[1] It was the architect's first commission outside of Japan where he was established as a designer of museums. Taniguchi worked on many museums in Japan, but most significant to MoMA's redesign is the architect's Marugame Genichiro-Inokuma Museum of Contemporary Art in Muragame City and, especially, the exterior of the Gallery of Horyuji Treasures in Tokyo; the interior creates physically one of the darkest museum experiences in recent museum architecture, quite the opposite of MoMA. However, in the Gallery of Horyuji Treasures there can be witnessed analogous solutions to what the architect has achieved for MoMA. In contrast to the visual overload and physical density of both Tokyo and New York, Taniguchi uses minimalism to produce an effect of calm, a playful sense of the inside and outside of the building, and, above all, an interplay of solid and void which is illustrated particularly in the similarity of the Gallery's façade and MoMA's rearticulated museum garden (which also reboots Philip Johnson's original layout from the 1950s): a huge emptied box that remarkably gives rectilinear shape to the void of the garden below.

MoMA is a prestigious site of "high culture", an institution that won and enjoyed global pre-eminence owing in part to the significance of its collection, in part to its geographical location and metropolitan status, and in part to the uniqueness of its mission (which might be boiled down to Ezra Pound minus the fascism). It defined the idea of the modern; it made the modern prestigious. In the following, I analyse the shift from its dictatorship of modernist aesthetic value to "the contemporary" as phrase, slogan, and organisational concept, in recent years after the twin incredulities towards the modern and the postmodern. Above all, the focus on "the contemporary" indicates the need to rethink the current historical emergency. How has MoMA negotiated the world historical eclipse of the modern and the postmodern? Can it really break free from their problematics? If cultural institutions cannot build definition and direction, other, more authoritarian, more powerful figures will not hesitate to step in and impose their own interests. The inclusion of the term signifies MoMA as part of a complex and vast system over which it has no control, but over which it will try to exert definitional effort nonetheless (as we will see). The reconstruction of MoMA tells us that it remains an authoritarian institution, but it is hardly *authoritative*.

## Controlling Institutions

MoMA's influence cannot be underestimated in its promotion of the Western sense of "the modern" in twentieth century culture. It gave strong definition to modern art, and by extension, the idea of modernity. It has loomed large in the imaginations of multiple generations. It is *not* shaping up to have the same amount of influence in terms of the contemporary, which may have something to do with the shapeless hesitations of "the contemporary" attitude itself. There have been times in which "modern" meant contemporary and vice versa—for instance, in the deployment of the contemporary in the late 1920s and 1930s by the Harvard Society for Contemporary Art, which can be viewed from the vantage of today's present as a key site of the intellectual origins of the Museum of Modern Art, preceding its opening by nine months.[2] Other precursory, proto-institutional moments of modernist history remain the Vienna Secession of 1897, the New York "Armory Show" of 1913, and also the controversy over Duchamp's provocative readymade *Fountain* in 1917. The basic move of the 2004 MoMA has been to deploy the contemporary next to, and in juxtaposition with (rather than being superimposed onto), self-certain, official Modernism. The effect is that the once-synonymous status of the terms modern and contemporary is rendered past. Looking at the instituting of the modern and the contemporary at MoMA also demands a reflection on MoMA's difficult negotiation with the category of the postmodern, as well as, historically, the moments of emergence of the modern and the contemporary. These considerations will help lead us to a reading of the new architecture, which exemplifies the physical growth of the museum out of the confines of modernity and postmodernity, and into the brave new world of contemporaneity.

The aesthetic order of the modern came from within the authority of MoMA in New York. Its deep roots lie in the American cultural imaginary and its self-perception as a leader in the modern world, especially after the Second World War. The latent meanings of modern in this sense were "democracy", the "free market" (capitalism), and the "melting pot" of immigration. The contemporary exerts its force from the outside. There is nothing particularly original about MoMA opening galleries organised around "the contemporary". The MCAs preceded MoMA's strong use of the categories. They spread and grew up around the globe—a part of the process of the historical desynonymisation of the terms modern and contemporary. Contemporary (as we saw in chapter two) has always indicated a certain discursive frustration with

---

[2] An account of the Harvard Society by Sybil Gordon Kantor in *Alfred H. Barr Jr. and the Intellectual Origins of the Museum of Modern Art* (195–210) offers a detailed study of the museum's early context as well as a biography of Barr himself.

the modern. If the aura of MoMA grew as a spectre or site of origin in the modern, then in the contemporary, it weakens. MoMA joins the reigning order rather than challenges it, in a sense reversing its historical (modernist) mission.

The contemporary announced a present that was no longer satisfactorily served by the term modern. Within the modern era, New York was the centre from which many of the great postwar definitions emerged, distilled into "movements" and slogans by MoMA. Within the contemporary, MoMA has become a museum among museums, a dinosaur perpetuating a history of modernism now so large, diverse, and fragmented as to be unmanageable. Its power of control had already waned; as part of the "modern project", MoMA was unable to seize hold of and control the development of the most critical postmodernist art, which openly interrogated the very heart of modernism (captured in the journal *October*[3]).

MoMA was not historically prepared for the postmodern moment. Indeed, the postmodern was an attack on MoMA. The museum struggled to negotiate the critical developments of the postmodern, the most radical of which sought to negate commodification and reification (and thus, the museum itself as an entity). When Lyotard argued for the "war on totality" in *The Postmodern Condition*, MoMA, while merely a museum, must be grasped as belonging to this category of totality. One need only witness the fact that artists such as Andy Warhol (Pop Art) and Donald Judd (Minimalism) were brought into the collection—into the story of late or postmodern art— as late as the 1990s, when their historical, and market, value had become undeniable. Warhol was not given a MoMA retrospective until after his death, something of which the artist was aware, stating "It will take my death for the Museum of Modern Art to recognise my work" (Bockris: 354). The high

---

[3] *October* was responsible for tracing the rise of postmodernism in both art and theoretical discourse. It is certainly a more complete "museum" for the period when it comes to the postmodern and to theory from the late 1970s to the 1990s than MoMA ever could be.

postmodern anti-institutional movements of the 1960s and 1970s—anti-totalistic postmodern art designed to negate the conservative museum culture—proved even more unfathomable to MoMA.

The desynonymisation of the terms modern and contemporary was latent within the earliest debates in Europe regarding the quarrel between the ancients and the moderns. The quarrel between the moderns and the postmoderns followed. Now, we have seen a quarrel between the postmoderns and the contemporaries (hardly worthy of the term "quarrel", for the postmodern seems to have faded without a fight). In "the contemporary" lies a de-intensification of the postmodern, accompanied by an increased sense of the directionless nature of history. The crucial difference is that the postmodern defined itself in terms of a project, whereas the contemporary does not. Foster, in the design context, called the contemporary "part of the greater revenge of capitalism on postmodernism" and a "routinisation of its transgressions" (2003: 25). In this ethos, MoMA was suddenly repositioned to make a comeback and to regain its authority. This was MoMA's chance: a big mobilisation of capital, an extra-large expansion, and the reorganisation of the visitor's gaze around the historical binary of Modernism (relocated to the upper levels of the museum, floors four and five) and the Contemporary Galleries (which were to be foregrounded anew—not out of the way, but the first thing one encounters upon entry into the main galleries).

The contemporary, as it is widely used and hailed both outside and inside MoMA, offers the eerie promise of a return to the modern and, crucially, a sidestepping of the ever-difficult category of the postmodern.[4] One thinks especially of

---

[4] It was Rosalind Krauss' insight in *'A Voyage on the North Sea'* that the installation art that had become an institutional commonplace increasingly since the 1970s represented the colonisation of former critique by power, by capitalism. So-called Installation Art, then, is part of the hegemonic gaze of the contemporary, a strategy for control of the "expanded field" of sculpture and performance.

the full-scale attack on the institution of the museum in the 1960s and 1970s, in the movements of fluxism, land art, process art, performance, happenings, situationism, conceptualism, and site-specificity. The contemporary arrives after the exhaustion of the postmodern, and after the "return" of painting in the 1980s (with Köln as the vanishing art market mediator) and the rise of official installation art (which now has its own purpose-built spaces, of which the Tate Modern's industrial-gigantic Turbine Hall is a good example). MoMA's deployment of the contemporary is more replication of historical deployments of the modern than anything else—the strongest expression of which was absence: namely, MoMA's refusal to execute new architecture in any of the post-modern or neo-historical styles identified by Charles Jencks and Robert Venturi.[5] It is easy to miss the fact that the discourse of the modern battled for, and won, its prestige. For the contemporary, MoMA's situation was different, as the category in its new hegemonic mode was virtually readymade by the late 1990s. If the postmodern tolerated a renewed relation to the past as a simulacrum or supermarket of ornament (detested by Adolf Loos)—categories effectively banned under purist modernism—the contemporary has the positive feeling of re-centring on the here and now, however illusory that might be.

Previously at MoMA, "modern" had functioned; *it does not today*. In Barr's time, the term had not yet been resignified into history, and presumably had not yet earned the unfortunate associations it renders consensually in the critical

---

[5] MoMA's addition of Cesar Pelli's big residential tower in 1984, as well as being the first art museum to open its own shop in the 1960s, are responses to fiscal pressures and the threat to its existence, but are not really postmodern aesthetic expressions in the sense of "contaminated" versions of the modern; the tower is perhaps late modern or an expression of what Koolhaas called the "culture of congestion". At any rate, they are evidence of the creeping market economy and the commodification of hitherto uncommodified realms of culture (such as the museum) associated with the postmodern, and, as such, fit Jameson's paradigm of the "cultural logic of late capitalism", but are not postmodern architectural statements.

imagination today. The features are listed by Jameson in his discourse on the "maxims of modernity" (2002: 1–13). These include the aura of authoritarianism that accompanies that which was modern: a certain (bourgeois) masculinity and a phallocentricity (in Hélène Cixous' sense), the teleology of the aesthetic, the minimalism, its insistent difficulty (as described by Adorno), the "cult of the genius or seer", as well as the Euro-centralism of much that was modern (the teleology of the West). MoMA managed to survive "late" or postwar modernism and the postmodernism of the 1970s and 1980s that sought to critically challenge the aforementioned negative categories, and has now repositioned itself as a place that wishes to create, promote, and (perhaps especially) control the politics and aesthetics of contemporaneity.

MoMA was extremely late to institute the contemporary by name. The term was not foregrounded until the 2004 reconstruction and, as noted above, was spatially located in the exact place of the old Modernist Galleries (in the same air). To say that MoMA was late to the contemporary is to admit a paradox. At the same time, MoMA has been concerned since its founding with the contemporary; each of its previous major architectural expansions (1939, 1953, 1964, and 1984) attest to this. In 1929, instead of "the contemporary", MoMA deployed Modern, and the phrase on the sign hanging on 53rd street—"Art of our time"—meant exactly this. It is hailed as the museum that harnessed the cataclysm that was modernism (a post-facto term coined by Greenberg to cover the diverse range of progressive, forward-moving art before the Second World War, and probably to retro-justify his beloved abstract expressionism of the 1940s and 1950s) in art and culture. The modern indicated a culture of the present moment that looked with disgust towards the past; nostalgia was effectively banned. Victorian and neo-Victorian aesthetics were not modern, even if they once had been. MoMA tried, in an original and formulaic way (actually in a Hegelian way) to theorise and represent, painstakingly, the rise of modern art and modern culture from the 1880s in Europe onward. The latter started with the School of Paris and continued all the way up to the construction of the modern in America and the New World.

MoMA, while ostensibly concerned with the contemporary, in 1929, was not contemporary—meaning "Modern"—when it opened. If one looks closely at the time, the deployment of the modern was in fact not synonymous with that of the contemporary, as is often assumed, insofar as contemporary was thought to mean "living" art. The museum is often cast in retrospect as having helped revolutionise our perception of museums in general. The museum refocused on the present, but it was in fact already entrenched in the past. It was already stuck in non-contemporaneity and, more to the point, on the pre-avant-garde modern (progressive, but not avant-garde). The list of artists in the museum's inaugural loan exhibition proves this. Futurism and Dada, the most extreme proponents of modernist ideology, had already happened, but the museum's opening vision was firmly placed in the nineteenth century.[6] The artists were Van Gogh, Gauguin, Cézanne, and Seurat. Vincent Van Gogh died in 1890, Paul Gauguin in 1903, Paul Cézanne in 1906, and Georges Seurat in 1891. In other words, the inaugural museum show was already in a state of retrospectivity. "Modern" was already historical. This is further seen in the way the museum chose not to exhibit consequential modernist painting, such as Italian Futurism, Russian Constructivism, or even French cubism,

---

[6] The fact that MoMA began conservatively is unsurprising given the public status of *modern* in the United States at the time, even after "the Armory Show". In 1921, the Metropolitan Museum of Art exhibited a show of Impressionists and Post-Impressionists that was greeted with outrage. In some cases, modern art was seen as an extension of Bolshevik philosophy, "applied to art". According to John Updike, a four-page printed protest read: "The real cult of 'Modernism' began with a small group of neurotic Ego-maniacs in Paris who styled themselves "Satanists"—worshippers of Satan—the God of Ugliness" (2). Such protests stopped the museum from trying to further the cause of modern art in the 1920s, which helped to create the void that the founders of MoMA filled in 1929.

and certainly not totally revolutionary art of Dada and the *readymade*. These styles entered the museum decades later in works that looked furthest forward to our own post-abstract, post-painterly, and "post-medium" contemporaneity (Krauss 1999: 5-7). MoMA was in a challenging place, being both radical *and* conservative in its construction of modernity, occupying a site of ambiguity. The categories of the modern and the contemporary join up in the "machine art" exhibition, again in the "international style" exhibition (both of the 1930s), and once more in 1939 when MoMA chose to house itself in a Bauhaus homage of a building. (More on this below).

Up to the 1970s, MoMA oversaw the introduction of separate departments of photography, film, prints and drawings, architecture, and design, as well as its original devotion to the "high" arts of painting and sculpture. In recent decades, MoMA has ostensibly become contemporary, yet it continues to perpetuate the modern on many levels. For instance, it does this formally through its continuation of medium separation and through the further separation of departments. MoMA was the first museum to institute multi-departmentalism, but seems now to be the very last to accept the deconstruction of departments and mediums. The resistance to alter the essentially modernist departmental structuring of knowledge is perhaps the first sign of the *noncontemporaneity* of Taniguchi's MoMA (in Ernst Bloch's sense, meaning simultaneously present but non-synchronous). Its modernist infrastructure is the ultimate relic from a bygone era. It had, and still does have, departments that hone areas that are divided by medium. These are artificial, arbitrary divisions, premised on a Greenbergian notion of modernism as the coming to self-consciousness of mediums rather than Krauss' notion of the "post-medium condition" of the contemporary, which is characterised by "the international fashion of installation and intermedia work, in which art essentially finds itself complicit with a globalisation of the image in the service of capital" (Krauss 1999: 56).

At a time in which emulation of MoMA's historic mission to collect and display in a disciplined fashion the most advanced art of the time has increased dramatically—in America, Europe, Eastern Europe, Asia and elsewhere—the institution has had to find new ways to compete, often in the face of daring wealthy projects by new museum *auteurs*. In New York City alone, MoMA has, for much of the last century, had the competition of the Guggenheim Museum and the Whitney Museum of American Art (both founded in the 1930s) and, perhaps most threateningly, the Metropolitan Museum of Art (with which it once had a relationship in the form of selling off works as they became old). More recent developments include the P.S. 1 Contemporary Art Centre in Long Island City, Queens, which was co-opted by MoMA as a "contemporary branch" of itself, possibly as a way to attempt to *control* such a free agent. The emergence of the New Museum of Contemporary Art, founded in 1977, which reopened in downtown Manhattan in 2007 in a purpose-built museum building, presents a further demonstration of the triumph of the term "contemporary"—of its default status—and adds another aspect of pressure on MoMA. The New Museum's inaugural downtown exhibition, *Unmonumental*, emphasised the querying and critical, anti-heroic nature of the contemporary. All of these contextual forces, in the form of other and newer, or younger, museums, put the old MoMA in a strange situation; has it become too canonical (at a time in which canons have been widely discredited as imperialist fictions), too overtly conservative, and most of all, too *historical*? Has it become, as critics have suggested, the "Metropolitan Museum of Modern Art", and therefore obsolete? The category of "the contemporary" is itself subject to time and change, and it is by no means certain how long the category will remain meaningful. It seems inconceivable now, but it may eventually become a sign of the past (negated by the post-contemporary, given a weak afterlife as retro). By the time MoMA reconfigured its collection, the postmodern, as a category, had already waned and tired; indeed, it is unlikely the term was seriously considered as the slogan for foregrounding current art (even since

1970).

## Remaking MoMA

The concepts of the modern and the contemporary merged in modernity and have now been desynonymised institutionally in contemporaneity.[7] To its credit, MoMA is a site that has actively sought to incite a discourse on the contemporary. It is also a site that, whether desirable or not, must eventually give the contemporary definition and begin to say what the contemporary is—to shape the contours of how we think of contemporaneity and in turn to shape our thinking of epochs. MoMA's reconstruction is in continuity with its original project of providing large-scale historico-temporal pictures. MoMA does this from the vantage of its own authorial viewpoint (which has become historical). That this is an essentially arbitrary exercise does not reduce its power, meaning, or influence. It is in this sense that the museum's license (any museum) to seize control of how time is collectively imagined and how it is managed publicly (democratically, visible to all or any) becomes reified in cultural space, architecture, and narrative.

Rebuilding was, as always, speculative. In a brief review of the redevelopment, William J. Mitchell saw the key to

---

[7] Matei Calinescu, in *The Five Faces of Modernity,* gives an excellent account of the desynonymisation of "the moderns and the contemporaries": "We are unable to fix a date, but it seems reasonable to assume that 'modern' and 'contemporary' were not felt to be significantly different before the twentieth century, when the movement that we call modernism became fully self-conscious" (87). I support Calinescu's argument, but take it a step further by articulating the development of the desynonymisation of the postmodern and the contemporary, which was not a move open to the theorist when he was writing in the mid- to late 1970s. For Calinescu, the content of the contemporary was that of the postmodern (a category he kept away from until he added an extra chapter, "On Postmodernism", to the second edition of his book in the mid-1980s).

Taniguchi's form as a contrast between signal and noise. He recalled that "art is signal" and "context is noise" within the regime of modernist display (172), and argued that the Taniguchi building was designed to maximise the signal-to-noise ratio. The resulting galleries arrived "like iPods—sleek, upmarket machines for experiencing art, white boxes that conceal a lot beneath the surface and focus all your attention on what's displayed within a rectangular frame and what's coming in through your earpiece" (172). The aim was to renew, re-envision, and *remint* the museum's identity, its collection, and boost prestige at an uncertain moment in its evolution. In a time in which new museums are built and old ones modified and remodified every year, MoMA was faced with extinction unless it took action. The spectacle of new architecture and a focus on the contemporary were Taniguchi's basic armoury, including a new atrium so giant as to almost herald the return of nineteenth century salon-style art.

It is with the waning of the modern at MoMA and its refusal to institute the postmodern in mind that we look over Taniguchi's MoMA redesign, which was conceptualised in the mid-1990s at the height of globalism, and developed in the early 2000s. Taniguchi made his innovation clear in his "architect's statement". These kinds of statements are often little more than PR exercises but can be revealing because of the architects' strong uses of rhetoric. It is here that the postmodern and the contemporary begin to become desynonymised for MoMA. This had everything to do with MoMA's choice of architect. (As we will see later, the Koolhaas proposal, *MoMA, Inc*, would have made MoMA a fully self-conscious corporate and postmodern entity.) Taniguchi made his intentions clear immediately with respect to galleries and public spaces, which he considers to be the "core elements" in a museum:

> A variety of gallery spaces appropriate to MoMA's collection of twentieth-century masterworks as well as new galleries for the yet-unknown works of contemporary art is the first requirement for an expanded museum. (Elderfield 1998: 242)

The provision of space for "the contemporary" is, for Taniguchi, an ontological demand. The contemporary is a commitment *in* the contemporary to what *will* be contemporary. The appeal of Taniguchi's proposal to those with the power to choose MoMA's new architect lay to a great extent in the fact that Taniguchi wanted MoMA to tell its story backwards, as it were, so that instead of starting with the modern and narrating "forwards" to the contemporary, the exhibit should start with the contemporary, with the newest and the latest, and only then begin to reveal how the culture of art arrived at this point in history. Taniguchi is credited therefore with urging the museum to demonstrate its commitment to contemporary art architecturally—which is to say, experientially—by placing it up front.

Taniguchi's usage also reveals a focus on the future, an openness to those works "as-yet-unknown": presumably meaning not-yet created works of art, possibly also indicating undiscovered works from the expanded globalist field. It is a Utopian conception in the strict sense of Ernst Bloch, meaning openness to that which has "not-yet" occurred (Bloch's term), an openness to that which we are not physically placed to possess as knowledge (which is to say the radical effacement of our own material present and ourselves). In his statement, Taniguchi reveres the ideal of the introduction of a difference—a present that is other to our own. This said, however, the architect's use of the contemporary denies the idea that one foot might be lodged in the world of tomorrow. For him, it may not be "progress", but expansion lies with the contemporary. If MoMA is impotent today it is not because it has failed to deploy contemporaneity (which is what Smith argued: "Has the Museum met the challenges of showing contemporary art? ... no way" [2005: 3]), but because it has failed to do *something else*. In 1997, Rem Koolhaas and the Office for Metropolitan Architecture did propose something else. Taniguchi, and Lowry as well, perceived contemporaneity, like globalism, as inevitable. In acting on their perception of the inevitable they have brought the merely possible into being. The foregrounding of the contemporary admits a globalist scale, but when we turn to the exhibited art works, we see that it has sided, mostly, with the Americans and the British (in the 2004-5 configuration): Bruce Nauman, Gordon Matta-Clark, Jeff Koons, Rachel Whiteread, Jeff Wall (in fact, a Canadian), and Gary Hill (to name only the most celebrated). The big story of the modern and the contemporary, for MoMA, remains that of a historical shift from the School of Paris to American postwar art.

We know that the discourse of contemporaneity is loaded with arbitrary dates of all kinds. The museum in its official literature has tried to clear up any historical questions about when the modern gave way to the contemporary by saying it all occurred in "approximately 1970" (Lowry: 34). What we have here is the deployment of a starting date: the myth of a profound beginning. It is, above all, a generational one—the generation of 1968, which was arguably the most radical of the postwar generations. MoMA has instituted the historical and imaginative limit of the generation of 1968 and the 1970s. But it is not today's limit. (Interestingly, this is also the year date used by the Victoria and Albert Museum in its "Postmodernism" show of 2011 (covering 1970-1990). MoMA, then, only erases the postmodern as a specific critique by structuring the beginnings of "the contemporary" back to 1970.)

Lowry's comparisons are bombastic, alluding to The British Museum and the Metropolitan. "The British Museum, for example, founded in 1753 ... is still today the embodiment of the Enlightenment belief in the universality of human experience" (Lowry 2005: 10). Characteristically, Lowry presents and repeats the undeconstructed idea of "Enlightenment", just as he does modern and contemporary, without registering its latent, yet core project for European or American imperialism, which one finds on the dialectical underside of these once attractive (an aspect attributed due to being seemingly safe and egalitarian) concepts. Lowry casts MoMA's project in continuity with the grand narrative of museums of imperialist definition: "The Metropolitan Museum of Art is a living testament to the attempt to present an encyclopaedic overview of art history to a nascent American audience" (Lowry 2005: 10). MoMA, he affirms, marks a difference:

> As for the Museum of Modern Art, the desire to provide a detailed but clearly intelligible history of modern art structures almost everything it does. But this desire is tempered by the reality—long recognised by the Museum—that it can never achieve this goal in any enduring way, since modern art is still unfolding and its history is still being written. (Lowry 2005: 10)

This claim is designed to reposition MoMA to develop the contemporary. It is a very open statement that seeks to legitimise investment in still incomplete aesthetic modernity, and thus in contemporaneity. At the same time, the museum knows its authority; through display, the museum has the power to authorise artists, works, concepts, narratives, to actively promote these phenomena into history, to create the necessary "buzz", and above all, to transform or reconstruct through these processes *art into capital*. The aura of the museum, the museum's architecture, and its history, all contribute to the suspension of the fact that the contemporary in the museum is as much a part of the general institution of contemporary art, which is a market of luxury goods. The museum, in this sense, is part of what Adorno and Horkheimer called the "culture industries" (Adorno: 131) where "distinction" (Pierre Bourdieu) is available for purchase. It is the museum's aim (perhaps even responsibility) to manufacture contemporaneity, to shelve and display it as well as imagine it, and above all, to try to control it through reification.

Lowry returns to Barr's old notion of MoMA as a laboratory of continual experiment. For Lowry, the contemporary is equal to telling the story of modern art, and "contemporary" is grasped as part of the paradigm of the high modern, as opposed to Foster's more troubling, and more serious, paradigm-of-no-paradigm. Lowry argues for "continuity", effectively papering over the challenges of the postmodern towards the end of the twentieth century. He wants the contemporary to be something desirable but uncontroversial, and not too political. This is a difficult aim. It is a timid position for a museum that is so well placed and resourced to create the aesthetic ontology of the present. (This reading should be understood via post-structuralism in which museums are thought to *create* our very idea of reality rather than passively *reflect* an unproblematic, fixed outside, historical, or contemporary world.)

In naming the contemporary, MoMA seeks to create a set of limits or controls for the term; that is, to prescribe what it may be and what it may not be. It is a governing apparatus, a gatekeeper. It is, then, a far cry from pretending to suspend authority. The author, MoMA *as auteur*, is here in full force. It also cannot be isolated from the attempt to marshal new objects in a practice that is essentially one of value adding. What the museum does is inseparable from the creation of capital; art is capital, past and present. The argument about the circulation of art in the service of capital and art as capital, within the bank-like structures of contemporary museums (the Guggenheim in Berlin was literally housed inside the Deutsche Bank), is developed by both Stallabrass in *Art Incorporated* and Paul Werner in a highly personal text (it reflects Werner's time, a lifetime no less, spent working as a guard on the floor of the New York Guggenheim), *Museum, Inc.* Both texts are essentially Marxist (Adornian) critiques of the de-differentiation of art and capital in "the contemporary".

The question of reconstruction involves the issue of creating periods of time. This is an inevitable issue for MoMA or any museum that wishes to represent movements of history. We looked at Lowry's demarcation. The late Kirk Varnedoe, former curator of painting and sculpture at MoMA, argued for "the contemporary" to be read back into the modern as continuation rather than profound, earth shifting change. In the introduction to his 2001 book *Modern Contemporary*, Varnedoe puts contemporaneity's beginning at 1980. For the purposes of that publication, Varnedoe opted to exclude work from the 1960s and 1970s in order to focus on what he called the museum's "contemporary acquisitions", which the public had had few opportunities to view, the "least known part of the Museum's collection", meaning art in the "period after 1980" (Varnedoe: 11). With reference to Barr's torpedo, Varnedoe argues that had the torpedo ideology been followed *strictly*, in which once-contemporary works were to be sold off to the Metropolitan when they showed signs of age (in other words when they became "classics"—Barr's scope was around fifty years), the earliest works in MoMA today would be from the 1950s. (Today they would be from the 1960s). The 1950s was the moment in which the museum decided to retain its collection of late nineteenth-century post-impressionist paintings, which had been keenly eyed by the Metropolitan. From the 1950s onward, Barr's torpedo becomes forever pinned to the 1880s as its starting point (Varnedoe: 12). For Varnedoe, "the revolutions that originally produced modern art, in the late nineteenth and early twentieth centuries, have not been concluded or superseded" (12). "Thus contemporary art today", he writes, "can be understood as the ongoing extension and revision of those founding innovations and debates" (12). The latent implication in these statements is that the postmodern has waned; at the postmodern's headstrong moment, such a position—the ongoing extension of modernism—would have been difficult to declare. Within the paradigm of "the contemporary", the modern is again available as a cultural resource.

The narrative breaks between the modern, the postmodern, and the contemporary are revised continuation. Contemporary art is folded back into modern art itself, which is a big and incomplete story. Varnedoe summons modern art as *the* ideology of contemporary art, as if contemporary art could not generate its own ideology (or as if it were not postmodern), but instead must rely on the industrial past. Recalling Jameson, we can read this as a part of the cultural "regressions of the current age": namely, the "reminting of the modern, its repackaging, its production in great quantities for renewed sales in the intellectual marketplace" (Jameson 2002: 7). At Taniguchi and Lowry's reconstructed MoMA, we find the modern repackaged, and the contemporary packaged to function in unproblematic continuity with modernism. Modernism once again becomes big business if it can function to add value to the contemporary and inscribe its presence through history. But MoMA's own past (meaning the collection of modern itself), outside of the "real" historical process, must not be mistakenly understood as static, because the process of acquisition and collection proceeds into the present day. Obviously enough, this is also true of past decades. Varnedoe states:

> [T]he institution began conservatively, and got more "progressive" as it aged. In the mid-1930s the Museum of Modern Art looked more like a museum of Kolbe, Maillol, and Pascin; it became the museum of Picasso, Matisse, Malevich, and Duchamp only gradually—often by key purchases made with the benefit of considerable hindsight. The purchase of Picasso's 1907 *Les Demoiselles d'Avignon* in 1937 is one example, the acquisition of key Abstract Expressionist works in the 1970s another; and several key works of the late 1950s and 1960s—by artists such as Rauschenberg, Warhol, and Judd—were only brought into the collection in the 1990s. (Varnedoe: 13)

The lateness of the acquisitions seems astounding. The museum has deployed the contemporary in its display of art "since 1970", its initial attempt to give definition to contemporaneity, but also in the new building itself. The strongest sign therefore of contemporaneity—apart from the term—is the architecture and its effect to re-invigorate an aging museum for a new population of art consumers. In this sense, the reconstruction is a strategy of survival, a fight against obsolescence, and ultimately the creation of new subjects of art history—indeed, of History itself. Jameson's capitalised version of History, based on the Lacanian Real, positioned history as inaccessible to us except through the interpretation of texts; history had become textual. The USD858 million reconstruction project, then, comes into the realm of the Nietzschean "will to power"—a healthy and competitive attempt to enter the museum market of official Contemporary Art (with capitals), bolstered by its Modern collection, which remains unsurpassed. Lowry came to the museum in 1995, its sixth director, and revealed his interest in carrying the museum onward to public spectacle, which he has succeeded in doing in a contradictory way. Under his reign, Taniguchi was deployed to execute an inconspicuous building, going against the grain set up by Thomas Krens and Frank Gehry in Bilbao, which brought the singular spectacle of the museum building—what Venturi and Scott-Brown called a "monumental duck"—into a renewed era of celebration.

## BIGNESS

The decision to reorganise the museum around the binary of modern and contemporary is evident in the actual finished design of the museum; walkable space (the physical separation of Modernism and Contemporary Galleries) is the most manifest expression, followed by which artists, artworks, and aesthetic groupings are found in those spaces. The museum used the terms "Modernist Galleries" and "Contemporary Galleries" and, to reinforce the separation, located them on different floors, thereby remanifesting and embodying the distinction in actual, designed space. The expansion signifies this distinction on many levels. The contemporary constitutes its own episteme ("1970 to the present"). The contemporary exceeds the modern (two floors, 1880-1940 and 1940-1970). The contemporary potentially includes the postmodern but is not limited to it ("1970-present"). The museum is untroubled in the deployment of the term, used everywhere in the wider field of the institutions to signify the art of the present. (It does not challenge the term. It conforms to it.) The museum is not aiming to differentiate itself from the horde of MCAs.

The museum is experiencing the same limit as the now-global MCAs. The museum is less a genuine attempt to represent the past than it is a conspicuous display of élite objects, many of which were paradoxically created with critical intentions but have now been colonised, superficially, by the commodity system, spectacle, and the bottom line of record numbers of museum visitors.[8]

A key aspect of Lowry's accomplishment at the museum has been in expanding the museum's audience and the scale of the building, to accommodate the newly minted mass of art consumers. Foster has suggested that as museum contents get uploaded into digital archives (an extension of André Malraux's concept of the *musée imaginaire* or "museum without walls") and are consequently more available than in previous eras, the experience of the museum building itself takes on a heightened significance. The museum must offer something that visitors will not get elsewhere. The museum building must become a spectacle, both as a singular experience in physical space and "as an image to be circulated in the media in the service of brand equity and cultural capital" (Foster 2003: 82). The museum was, Lowry writes, "born of a fundamental conviction that modern art (that is, the art of our time) is as exciting and important as the art of the past, and that the pleasures and lessons of engagement with it should be as large as possible" (Lowry 2005: 13). It almost sounds as if Lowry had been reading Koolhaas' manifesto on "Bigness" and taking it literally; make the audience bigger, the building bigger, the returns bigger. This is the story of the reconstruction of MoMA, which basically equalled an altogether new building—almost doubled in size—to register its commitment to "the contemporary", all part of a real or imagined connection to the revolutions of a hundred or so years ago.

The museum's new atrium, at 110 feet, exemplifies the ideology of Bigness. This extends throughout most of the second floor galleries, which are double height and are the ones

---

[8] The tourist population which went down in the post-9/11 depression has long since gone up again.

designed to accommodate the contemporary. Foster noted this expansion in his review of the museum: "the Contemporary Galleries ... are large enough to contain King Kong in the next remake" (2004: 24). The museum was planned and constructed on a narrative of contemporary art as something that was getting larger all the time. Richard Serra was seen as the paradigm and the precedent, or anticipation, of the future. Serra's cor-ten steel sculptures are often described with the epithet "architectural" because they are large "walk-in" works of minimalism; they demand a bodily exercise from their viewer, as the shifting perspectives of the works are only permitted by the viewer's own movement and experience. For MoMA, architecture became the site for imagining the future. If we read the space of the completed building we must conclude that the curators, director and architect, believed that the future of the contemporary was on an inevitable course of ever larger works. This was a perception that broke significantly with Barr's original vision of the museum as being organised around apartment-sized rooms; such rooms were radical, for Barr, because they presupposed a bourgeois art that was affordable, spontaneous, and accessible to general ownership, in rejection of the overlarge salon paintings of the nineteenth-century which were élitist by comparison. The new atrium signifies a turn away from the old apartment-sized rooms, which are retained on the fourth and fifth floors in the Modernist Galleries. This confidence in the future Bigness of art was a perception not limited to those at MoMA. Its excitement was also that of Frank Gehry/Thomas Krens' venture in Bilbao, the Tate Modern's Turbine Hall, Mass MoCA (Krens again), and DIA: Beacon in New York State.

The path by which the museum arrived at the contemporary, but did not arrive at the postmodern—terminologically, at the most public level—is not difficult to trace. The contemporary was suddenly used in the Taniguchi remake, whereas the postmodern has never been officially deployed in the foreground at the museum. What we see is that "the contemporary" is not the value-free zone that it wants to be, always trying to be one step ahead of the oppression called history. However, neither is it a straightforward carrying-on of modern or postmodern under the guise of a new term exploited for its relatively association-free quality (as opposed to the modern and postmodern, which have ideologically heavy associations). Certainly, the immense dilation in the sphere of museums of contemporary art at the end of the century seems to fall into that critical perspective of the postmodern that understands the culture as one of the flattening out of the modern, as Jameson insisted (1991: 306), whereby the once élite culture of the moderns is suddenly available—democratised, or to use Bertolt Brecht's term, "plebeianised". Inevitably, this entails a thinning out of its critical substance; indeed, commercialisation makes distribution possible in the first place. In the contemporary, we see an instituted critical art, but a critical attitude without commitment to a metanarrative, teleology, or a future *as anything different from that which already exists.* The narrative of the time is one of the replacement of hierarchy with accumulation and composition with addition. To quote Koolhaas, playfully modifying Mies van der Rohe ("Less is more") for the age of super-capitalism, the slogan of MoMA today must indefatigably be, "More and more, more is more" (2004a: 163). Those in charge of the project did not go so far as to *rename* the museum, which would have been suicide given its brand and recognition value, but the decision to include and internally foreground the term "contemporary" is symptomatic of the broader urban ethos in which the establishment now finds itself, which is global and digital. Let us now look at the corporate and architectural context of Taniguchi/Lowry's MoMA.

## MODERNISM'S CORPORATE HEADQUARTERS

The boom in museums and institutes of "the contemporary" is paralleled by the Guggenheim Museum's emergence as a global brand in the 1990s and its remarkable transformation into a franchise under director Thomas Krens. (His years as director were 1988-2008). The role that architecture has played within this process is astounding. Although MoMA did not go down the path of Krens' to turn itself, like the Guggenheim, into a franchise (it is, however, certainly a "brand"), the super-capitalist era for MoMA has seen the museum strike deals with large corporations. For instance, JP Morgan Chase Bank, Ford Motors, Banana Republic, and Target have recently supported MoMA. Finance capital and the oil, motor, and clothing industries can be read not as separate entities, but as corporate parts of the museum itself, parts of the museum's overall latent (invisible) content and integration into American culture.

The Guggenheim Museum's expansion illustrates the most visible turn to corporate culture within museums, and might be read as part of American culture's long Cold War triumph. The Guggenheim has seen an age of its multiplication, adjusting itself to life in the global economy. Michael Brenson has argued that the phenomenon is a part of America's expansive, ideological confidence in a world reduced to the imagination of capitalism (Brenon 2002: 5). Much has been written already on its proliferation, notably Brenson's pamphlet, *The Guggenheim, Corporate Pluralism, and the Future of the Corporate Museum* and John Loughery's essay "The Future of Museums: The Guggenheim, MoMA, and the Tate Modern". These usefully draw connections between each of the museums' new business functions. Both accept the exceptional talent and vision of Krens but are critiques of a museum culture that, in Loughery's words, has become "more concerned with real estate than art" (631). Branches of the Guggenheim museum can now be found in Berlin, Venice, and, most famously, in Bilbao, Spain. In 2001, an ambitious branch designed by Koolhaas opened in Las Vegas in the Venetian (an oversized hotel-casino complex) but did not last and closed in 2003. A Guggenheim-Hermitage gallery, not as ambitious as the Guggenheim, also opened in the Venetian Hotel, which continues today. At the end of the 1990s, a proposed Guggenheim Museum was planned for New York's East River (designed by Gehry), an impressive and gigantic Bilbao-looking docked sea creature from the depths of the ocean (the depths of the unconscious), but construction was called off after the events of September 11, 2001.

Four more Guggenheims have been proposed, which only serves to strengthen the case for the intoxication of the institution with globalism: one for Guadalajara, Mexico; one for Bucharest, Romania; Zaha Hadid has won the competition to design a Guggenheim-Hermitage in Vilnius, Lithuania; and a Helsinki Guggenheim competition has been a recent focus for the architectural spectacle. Add to this already complex picture the Guggenheim under construction in Abu Dhabi. Designed by Gehry, it is slated to be, as everything in the pre-money crash UAE was to be, the *largest* Guggenheim Museum in the world, and will be located next door to the new Louvre "satellite" museum (the first Louvre satellite/franchise). The large and the extra-large are, from Starbucks Coffee and indoor ski-slope to shopping mall and Hotel Atrium, Dubai and Abu Dhabi's inaugural "style" (or, arguably, a substitute for style).

The recent era of the distribution of "the contemporary" furnishes us with a history of plundering the world beyond MoMA and New York. In other words, not unlike the original Frank Lloyd Wright Guggenheim, MoMA was once a special, one of its kind museum: an avant-garde cultural apparatus. MoMA today goes on, but it does so in the context of a mass of museums that has mimicked that historical museum's effort. The foundation of similar museums in its long twentieth-century wake served to enhance MoMA's aura. Michael Kimmelman, writing in the *New York Times*, called it the "corporate headquarters of modernism" (2004: 35). This diagnosis of the museum as corporate is a way of signifying the museum's impotence, of pointing to its non-antagonistic, now *defused* modernist nature. MoMA represents a modernism without its Utopian agenda: an emptied out, non-teleological modernism. John Updike, in his *New Yorker* review, gestured towards the same when he noted, "It has the enchantment of a bank after hours" (2004: 1). MoMA can be said to have inaugurated a phenomenon, but is no longer at the helm of that phenomenon. The Guggenheim can more accurately be said to be at the helm of the exploitation by museums of globalism and the belief that wider and wider distribution is inevitable—as far as capitalism can reach.

MoMA had grown up as a breakthrough twentieth-century institution, as a true centre of culture, founded by Abby Aldrich Rockefeller, Lillie P. Bliss, and Mary Quinn Sullivan, at a time in which "the modern" was still a building concept, not an established cultural phenomenon. Since then, however, the place for contemporary art museums has come to seem virtually limitless the world over; existing in the old rich countries, but also those recently opened to big capital (in Eastern Europe as well as parts of Asia, and now the Middle East). If the so-called "Bilbao-effect" has created anything, it has created desire where there was none before—a massive historical expansion in desire. It is a desire for contemporaneity; although, increasingly, the Bilbao-effect has become the Bilbao-syndrome, wherein a frenzy of singular-sculptural or technological buildings are constructed, each city assuming that the investment will inevitably be regenerative. Within globalism there is a notion—an ideology—that one only need "build it and they [the masses] will come". What we witness in the most extreme cases of the Bilbao-syndrome is a short-term, event-oriented architecture, the creation of a temporary global centre, like a blockbuster film that must recover its investment within the first week. A good deal of the work in this sort of contemporary architecture lies in marketing, publicity, hype, and image development.

Contrary to this picture of the lavish development of "the contemporary", the construction of the concept of the contemporary—its gaining of momentum and building of confidence—has in another, different capacity gone on outside of the New York MoMA (and high finance projects such as the Guggenheim), often at small, independent, occasionally short-lived and usually marginal museums, galleries, and artist-run initiatives (ARIs). These smaller projects have not had the pressure of a constant expansion in audience size, and have in consequence tended to be more daring and experimental.

## Paradoxical Minimalism

Hal Foster writes of the remake, "abstraction still rules, but it is not the pictorial-spiritual variety of the *White on White* of Malevich—it is architectural-financial" (2004: 25). Modernist, for Foster, has been reduced to mean "Minimal", and implies a dematerialisation associated rightly with a reversal of what these terms used to mean. Minimal once meant the exposure of technique and material, the foregrounding of function, and modernist meant the following through of functions in the elaboration of forms (according to the slogan "form follows function"). In the deployment of Taniguchi, for Foster, illusion is back. Taniguchi is reported to have said to the trustees: "Raise a lot of money for me, I'll give you good architecture. Raise even more money, I'll make the architecture disappear" (Foster 2004). This statement was circulated and endlessly repeated in the media as the explanatory position of Taniguchi on his redesign: a disappearing act.

Foster's argument reminds us too that MoMA's history goes beyond that of the museum, its trustees, its curators, and the collection, into the realm of the past and History itself. History, for Foster, as for any Marxist, is ultimately one great collective force, driven by contradiction. MoMA's past hints at enmeshment to the twentieth century's conflicts, tensions, liberations, wars, mass deaths, repression, overthrows, and despair. Foster writes:

> MoMA still offers little sense of the great events of the 20th century, or of the entanglements of Modernism with Fascism, totalitarianism, Fordism, mass culture and capitalist spectacle. Perhaps the first task of such a museum is formalist—to highlight the intrinsic properties of each work and the internal development of each art—but that needn't be the only task. Like some others, I had hoped (even expected) some space to be used to evoke more context: why not a presentation that points to cultural prob-

lematics and historical conjunctures, and brings other kinds of objects, images and documents into play ... As it is, an old pedagogy is weakened and a new one has not yet emerged. (2004: 24)

It is possible that Mario Perniola's notion of an "Egyptian pedagogy" succeeds the modernist pedagogy of which Foster speaks. Such pedagogy has arguably been deployed in the Museum of Old and New Art (MONA) in Tasmania, which combines artefacts from the ancient and the contemporary together as "contemporaries" within that installation; a mummy in close proximity to a Kandinsky, and nearby, a Damien Hirst spin painting. The combination of old and new seems to offer a dialectical displacement to the stalemate of homogenous contemporaneity or strict linear progression in hegemonic art museum culture, but could as easily be grasped as an all-in, uncritically inclusive contemporaneity.

Given the right "hermeneutic bomb" (Smith 2001: 5), the discussion could turn toward repressed cultural problematics cited by Foster. But MoMA functions to give all of what was subversive about historical modernism an air of respectability. The fascist element, which is everywhere in the writings of many first-wave modernists (Marinetti obviously, but also Pound, Eliot, Lewis et al), can get lost in the sentimental effect of the museum context.[9] Awe in the face of the objects of art

---

[9] Paul Virilio makes the connections clear in his *Art and Fear*. He cites Richard Hulsenbeck, a leading German Dadaist, speaking to a Berlin audience in 1918: "We were for the war. Dada today is still for war. Life should hurt. There is not enough cruelty" (29). He cites Filippo Marinetti's slogan for Italian futurism around 1909: "War is the world's only hygiene" (29), which leads, as Virilio rightly pointed out, "directly, though thirty years later ... to the shower blocks of Auschwitz-Birkenau" (29–30). Several more fascist or proto-fascist sympathies are brought up and cited by Virilio. According to Hulsenbeck: "*Dadaism demands* ... The international revolutionary union of all creative and intellectual men and women on the basis of radical communism" (1998: 256)

replaces the confrontation of who we are and where we have come from, and what the twentieth century may have been about. This is a basic problem of the "laboratory conditions" of the white box display, as a form—the hegemonic modernist exhibition mode. Foster argues against the *sterilizing* tendency of MoMA, which is a technique carried over from high modern thought and also from the practices of modern science (hence Pound's metaphor of laboratory conditions [1960: 23]). Taniguchi and Lowry were under no obligation to choose continuity over rupture. Foster would have preferred to see an intervention rather than an endorsement of the establishment, a change in direction. He is critical of any tendency to smooth out rupture in the deployment of the twentieth century:

> Between the fifth and fourth floors the P&S presentation breaks at 1940, as do most courses in 20th-century art; this break tacitly accepts the hiatus produced by Fascism, World War Two and the Holocaust—repression, exile and death—and the brochure for the fourth floor does cite Adorno on the near impossibility of lyric poetry after Auschwitz. Yet, again, you wouldn't know these events had occurred, and in this regard too the new MoMA is in keeping with the old. Within its affirmative story is a historical silence that might be fundamental to postwar reconstruction, in which (to put it crudely) the recovery of Modernism in the form of 'the Triumph of American Painting' is offered up as cultural compensation for the devastation of Europe. (Foster 2004: 24)

The feeling of the obscure flattening out of History expressed by Foster is only exacerbated by Taniguchi's refusal to break out of the paradigm of the modernist white box. Foster admits that the opening exhibit—"the hang"—was not permanent; it has since been reconfigured several times—a hallmark of the flexible, arbitrary nature of "the contemporary".[10]

---

[10] For Foster, the hang was seemingly too random, with peers (in

As MoMA shows, "the contemporary" is a site of power in itself. This does not mean that the contemporary is not critical, but that its critique is readily housed within the centre of the spectacle: the museums—the exact place that used to be the object of attack for the most radical of the moderns and the postmoderns. For MoMA, the reconstruction was a chance to create its own space for the contemporary and to give identity to non-identity. Smith, writing in Australia's *Art Monthly*, criticised the entire layout of the museum for sidling up against the leading commercial architecture of our time. For him, Taniguchi's redesign turns out to be, without really trying to hide the fact, a themed mall or entertainment centre, at least in basic concept. The massive atrium, with its 110 foot high ceiling is what led Smith to this association:

> The main floor is nailed down at its centre by Barnett Newman's *Broken Obelisk* 1963-69 ... Although this sculpture is one of the few works in the collection that could survive in such a space, it establishes immediately a double message: Modern Art is iconoclastic—see how we endorse the artist's attack on classicism—but don't you love *how* he does it—such *élan*, such risky solidity, such authority. Here we are. And there you are. Passing each other, comfortably, *en route* to the next art excitement ... this kind of messaging gets too close to a themed fountain in a mall or an entertainment centre. (2005: 4–5)

The very size of the reconstructed MoMA has more in common with that other massive interior space of the modern age, namely the shopping mall, than it does the traditional museum; certainly, it shares the necessary technological pre-

importance as well as age) separated between the modern and the contemporary with no rationale. This is a product of the physical separation of the galleries into ultimately arbitrary, or generationally contingent, eras. For example, Robert Smithson and Bruce Nauman are in modern galleries, whereas Richard Serra and Gordon Matta-Clark are in the contemporary.

conditions—air conditioning (which Rem Koolhaas once said "launched the endless building" (2004a: 162)) and the escalator, with its enormous consequences for building space. These factors are not new to the Taniguchi version of the building (they were part of the very aesthetic in Cesar Pelli's 1984 incarnation) but they do help to intensify, and render possible, the experience of Bigness that Taniguchi has helped bring into being for MoMA in the age of contemporaneity.

The atrium, Smith suggests, delivers its audience to what is typical of most postmodern foyers and multiplexes: a "mixture of disorientation and directedness" (2005: 4–5). It is perhaps not unlike the postmodern hotel (for Jameson, in one of his science-fictional moments), the Westin Bonaventure in L.A., which represents, for him, a mutation in space that has not yet found its equivalent mutation in the human subject (1991: 44). A "mutation" of this order may be occurring in relation to fine art at the new MoMA, in which a mutation in art exhibition space has not yet found its equivalent in contemporary art itself. Or, a more convincing argument would be that the atrium of Taniguchi's MoMA offers us an alarming disjunction between the scale of modern and modernist art and its built environment. This is a space designed to anticipate that which is yet to come, that which has not-yet arrived (harking back to Taniguchi's own statement and Bloch's Utopianism). Jameson writes of the Westin Bonaventure: "The newer architecture therefore ... stands as something like an imperative to grow new organs, to expand our sensorium and our body to new, yet unimaginable, perhaps ultimately impossible, dimensions" (1991: 39). On the other hand, it is entirely possible that the atrium, and huge contemporary galleries, is simply the institutional-spatial expression of the establishment's full endorsement of a particular, late, and very large form of sculptural practice, the closest of which might be the large sculptures of Richard Serra.

The size of the contemporary galleries is therefore suggestive of another disjuncture between the modern and the contemporary. Modernism's basic unit was the canvas suited to modern urban life and city mobility, with its manageable size and suitability for the modern apartment. Art's destination was not institutional; it was the private home. (The original of MoMA's galleries, right up until Pelli's redesign, were like ghost apartments.) Today, the museum challenges artists with the provision of space itself; can the artist create a work that will transcend this space—that is, not be swallowed by it whole? Is Koolhaasian Bigness not the default of the contemporary exhibition space? MoMA's atrium has been readied for the next phase of spectacle, the next part in the story of art's ability to attract crowds and also compete with the other culture industries, such as cinema, or the theme park itself; a market the museum entered with the introduction of its $20 (USD) entrance fee, which in 2004 made the museum the most expensive in the US. The museum has become the destination for contemporary art (or, in any case, it sees itself that way). Likewise, audiences have become more subject to commodification than before, the mark of which is perhaps the bar code (Universal Product Code) found on the back of every museum ticket scanned on entry into the museum; the information it rapidly provides the retailer potentially alters the whole planning, distribution, and quantity of goods or artworks on display. The more recent introduction of iPod Touch software and geotagging in museums offers another level of the digitalization/commodification of the museumgoer (such as at Tasmania's MONA), with unknown horizons.

Smith provides a phenomenology of walking through the space and analyzing the narrative of art's great transformations. Contemporary Art is his main area of concern (capitalised, to indicate its institutional approval), the challenges of which he reasonably believes MoMA refuses to live up to. Smith argues that "Contemporary Art lite" (2005: 8) is the dominant tone at the museum. He uses the term in homage to Stallabrass' "High Art Lite", which is used to describe the phenomenon of young British artists, or YBAs, in the 1990s. Stallabrass suggested using "high art lite" in preference to YBA and its cognates, "Brit art" and "new British art", because the latter are too confining for a tendency that he understands as not limited to Britain, but is potentially global. He writes in *High Art Lite*: "I hope that it captures the idea ... an art that looks like but is not quite art, that acts as a substitute for art" (Stallabrass 1999: 2). MoMA effectively works the same way, its contemporary galleries provide an art that looks like an avant-garde, but is in fact mostly pre- or pseudo-contemporary.[11]

Smith and Foster both critique the over-reliance given to Minimalism at the new MoMA. In Smith's argument, the inaugural installation functioned to stall and distort contemporary developments beyond Minimalism. MoMA's prejudices were revealed in the construction "Untitled (Contemporary)", which was the title used in MoMA's brochures and on its wall inside. Smith's point was that "the contemporary" was deployed literally as parenthetical in relation to Minimalism; the contemporary was as offered as a kind of *afterthought*. This evinces the museum's failure to go beyond late modern-

---

[11] The emergence of the YBAs was a major event informing the ideological formation of mainstream museum art in the twenty-first century that MoMA does not acknowledge. The YBA phenomenon was controversial for numerous reasons, not least of which was the role advertising mogul Charles Saatchi played in instituting what was essentially his own collection, and his own taste for "bad taste" (when Saatchi's exhibition *Sensation* finally came to New York, Mayor Rudolph Giuliani was particularly offended by Chris Ofili's elephant dung paintings), and especially of using branding and marketing techniques; for instance, the auction house Christie's was a sponsor to the show, which reduces the show to an explicit attempt to drive up value in the works. But, then again, MoMA has always underprivileged British art in its collecting. Still, it seemed like sheer rejection of current British art when *Sensation* was not held at MoMA, but instead at the Brooklyn Museum. The *Sensation* exhibition is indicative of the situation of art at the end of the century, especially if we are willing to develop a kinship between it and the notorious "Armoury show" of 1913. Not only did the show cause protest on opening as well as on closing, but also the museum famously felt it wise to include a Health Warning for visitors to the show: "the contents of this exhibition may cause shock, vomiting, confusion, panic, euphoria, and anxiety".

ism. Finally, Smith charged MoMA with not knowing, nor developing the mechanisms (growing new organs) to know, how to deal with internet art (also digital art, tech art, etc.), which has been discussed elsewhere by Stallabrass; beyond that is an original iPod included in a cabinet on the Design level. There is a Media Room but its collection is limited to film and video. MoMA may never register the "conditions of contemporaneity" and the values of the art produced within its paradigm—that is, not stylistically Modern but genuinely new and emergent, the *novum*. MoMA has more recently purchased a number of video games and the appropriate hardware to play them; this might be a hesitant step towards "the contemporary". But in fine art MoMA has remained tied to the Modern European past and its fulfillment in the American tradition, that is, to celebrating the now deep ancestry of one only (virtually national) aspect of contemporaneity.[12]

---

[12] MoMA remains tied to the past in another sense—that is, in its failure to acknowledge the wealth of women artists who have contributed to the story of modern and, especially, Contemporary Art. Jerry Saltz, then art critic of the *Village Voice*, complained rightly of the low-representation of women modern and contemporary artists in the new MoMA. This complaint continues the one made by rallying artists, critics and passionate visitors when the Cesar Pelli building was completed and MoMA reopened in 1984. A pamphlet from the Museum Archives reads: "Museum of Modern Art Opens: But NOT to women artists". Their demands were as follows:
- MoMA policy should reflect what is really happening in contemporary art and not simply what some dealers want to sell.
- Women artists have been in the forefront of the art movements since the 70s and 80s. We demand adequate representation for our work.
- We demand that MoMA:
    1) Exhibit women's work from the permanent collection.
    2) Feature women's work in loan exhibitions.
    3) Establish a policy for acquiring women's work.

According to the pamphlet: "Of 165 artists included in MoMA's inaugural exhibit for its new exhibition hall, only 14 are women artists.

The museum has been locked in displaying its own "spectacle value", as noted by Foster (2003: 81). The museum is reduced to reproducing itself as a list of chart toppers or greatest hits, which forfeits criticality for popularity and ease of consumption. This perspective ties into Smith's critique of the museum becoming a theme park. Jerry Saltz once made the point: "you can't develop what Oscar Wilde called the 'critical spirit' if you're mainly seeing masterpieces" (2005b).

MoMA still has much to teach. What it used to teach—the metanarrative of the torpedo—is what many postmodernists tried to escape, only to find one fine day all their critiques and complaints in a room nearby, absorbed by the additive logic of museums and bourgeois history generally. The modernist thinker Robert Scholes, in his work on the "paradox of modernism", summed up nicely the three key aspects of MoMA's thought:

1. Modernism *equals* Abstraction—"is essentially abstract".
2. Modernism is mainly Parisian, with Continental offshoots and American successors.
3. Figuration is a retrograde movement, going against the progressive tide that was flowing toward Abstract Impressionism. [sic] (2006: 93)

The deployment of "the contemporary" renders these elements as *past*, because the Hegelian inevitability-effect is lost in the present. Yet, the pedagogical value of MoMA still exists no matter how "corporatised" and "spectacular" it may have become in the minds of its early twenty-first century critics and its complicit architect and director. This position must be defended. The museum has always been a business first and foremost, a company that is explicitly in the business of running a museum of modern art. This is obvious. It is an institution of modernity—which is to say, of monopoly capitalism.

This exhibition is entitled 'An Exhibition Survey of Recent Painting and Sculpture.'"

But unlike standard capitalist companies, it occupies an unusual, ultimately defensible, position in society and culture: it is both *of* modernity and in critical response to the world historical phenomenon of modernity. It tries to tell us that modernity *did happen*, which is significant in itself, to borrow Huyssen's phrase, in a "culture of amnesia". The reminder that our current way of life, indeed our whole socio-economic system, is tentative, provisional, and contingent, remains the radical aspect of MoMA.

## Pluralism Reigns

What is especially interesting in the museum's use of architecture, within its history of constructing, expanding and reconstructing, is that at these junctions the museum is given its own moment for expression as opposed to the arguably more passive and consumptive practice of collecting and displaying. At each expansion, the building equals the institution's "most representative artifact, not something it had collected, but something it had created, the most potent signifier of its Utopian aspirations" (Wallach 1992: 208). The original MoMA building was designed by the architects Philip S. Goodwin and Edward D. Stone. It was homage to Walter Gropius' Bauhaus in Germany: clean lines and hard edges, a machine aesthetic that set up a conscious juxtaposition between itself and the surrounding nineteenth-century New York brownstones from the "backward" Victorian past. MoMA inverted its aesthetic environment to offer a future of "rationality, efficiency, and functionality" (Wallach: 208). MoMA was in what Wallach called its Utopian stage, which is the image of the museum within full and progressive modernity, before the querying of the "great collective project", before deconstruction, before the reign of plurality. The Taniguchi reconstruction is arguably the opposite of the Utopian; it is representative of a wholly complacent attitude towards that which exists. Taniguchi does not show us a way out.

In the discipline of architecture, MoMA has had a tendency within history to inaugurate and promote a style. It has given style definition through a process of discovery, celebration, and exhibition. Taniguchi registered another layer to this tendency that indicates the museum in a kind of loop of self-influence. It actively produces contemporaneity. Taniguchi writes:

> MoMA has in the past used the design of its built form as an opportunity to regenerate itself and to express what is current in the arena of modernism. As an integral part of the Museum's history, this record of regeneration should not be destroyed, but should be preserved and celebrated in the juxtaposition of past and present, the new or experimental contrasted to the known or established. (qtd. in Elderfield 1998: 242)

This is not a discourse on modernity. Taniguchi's terms register a respect for context, the past, and the already known as opposed to the new, the shocking, the revolutionary. Taniguchi opted for the preservation of historical facades from various earlier expansions and the reconstruction of Philip Johnson's Museum Garden: the same garden that Richard Serra recommended be the first thing "scrapped" in any redesign. Taniguchi's vision tended towards a relatively conservative *continuity*, the display or reframing of the "tradition of the new" rather than its concrete enactment. In deploying Taniguchi, the museum has opted for *restoration over revolution*. But no one today is going to be convinced by the full project of restoring the modern, which is an impossible task. What we are left with, then, is the shell of the modern: its façade, a hollowed out modernism, a modern that lacks a relationship to the future, one that sees the future as one of undiscontinued contemporaneity, which is by definition wholly distinct from the modernist future.

The history of MoMA's own major architectural exhibitions proves instructive. The Goodwin and Stone building (MoMA's first purpose-built structure) was executed in the "international" or Bauhaus style in 1939, which saw the museum materially (that is, spatially and architecturally) merge and become part of the Modern Movement architecture. Like abstraction in painting, the Modern Movement was seen as an irreversible, inevitable element of progress within democratic, secular, industrial societies which the United States aspired to at the time, and which Europe expressed, even more strikingly and disturbingly, in the "modernism" of its various fascisms. Architecture, in other words, was caught up in the intoxicating, consensual hallucination of the vision of linear forward development to which Barr's image of the torpedo gave the most succinct aesthetic articulation. In 1932, Philip Johnson, Henry-Russell Hitchcock, and Barr travelled in and surveyed "advanced" Europe. (Someone should make a film about that trip.) Shortly after, they held their show *Modern Architecture: International Exhibition* that showcased Modern Movement architectural concepts, drawings, scale models, designs, and ephemera. It was a summation of advanced work in architecture in the 1920s. The names of the architects in the show, the so-called "heroes", from Le Corbusier and Mies van der Rohe to Gropius and Jacobus Oud, testify to the overall aesthetic allegiance of MoMA: avant-garde, in the classic sense meaning future-oriented, hailing singular abstraction, and strictly following dictums such as "less is more". The show had great ambition; it was to result in the isolation of a new style that would, in a way comparable to International Gothic or Romanesque in their day, "take over the discipline of art" (Johnson 1988: 7).

MoMA's architecture, then, broke away from the royal hierarchies of aristocratic Europe, the palatial paradises built before the French Revolution. It was not a style appropriate to the Grecian or Roman nostalgia favoured by the Victorian bourgeoisie. Modern Movement architecture was supposed to shock the local bourgeoisie when it arrived in town, with its austere lack of ornament (which historically signified class, taste, and refinement), its brief against homeliness, and above all, its arrogant disrespect for context. "The Modern"—as the museum was affectionately called—instead offered a set of principles, techniques, even demands, all based on the technologies and newer materials of glass, steel, and reinforced concrete. The *Modern Architecture* show and the Goodwin and Stone building taken together formed a manifesto agitating for a different future architecturally, but also socially.

Taniguchi's redesign of the museum reveals a different kind of institution: one that has shifted position, but not radically. The expansion indicates the institution's deepened neoconservatism. Unlike the international style, which was hailed as the inevitable architecture to come, Taniguchi deployed minimalism as a stylistic choice out of the supermarket of architectural styles that were historically and ideologically open to him in the late 1990s. There is no sense of grand narrative present in Taniguchi's reasons. If anything, the deployment of minimalism reveals a return of the most conservative tradition: conserving the past for its own sake. In the words of Terence Riley, the curator of architecture at MoMA: "Taniguchi's design for the Museum of Modern Art must be seen as a response to the needs of a particular institution rather than a disembodied manifesto for museums everywhere" (Davidson 2005: 101). This attitude is not modernist; it is *also* not simply a case of postmodernism. Taniguchi's building neither epitomises modernism's ideals, wrapped into a singular statement of aesthetic authoritarianism, nor is it a critique of modernism that tries to demonstrate or mark modernism's critical failures.

The theorist and critic Cynthia Davidson compared Taniguchi's Japanese museum designs to the new MoMA, saying that the style was "eerily reminiscent of the new MoMA itself ... similarly free of critical architectural ideas and similarly resistant to criticism" (2005: 101). Davidson noted something other critics have omitted: the new architecture's conceptual and aesthetic relevance to the *Light Construction* exhibition, held in 1995, curated by Terence Riley (who was chief of architecture at MoMA at the time of Taniguchi's selection). Davidson argues that Riley's use of the word "manifesto" speaks to the institution's continued interest in the purchase of influence, or what is better called its ongoing authoritarianism. Davidson writes:

> Because Riley's statement comes at a time when the surfaces of "light construction" are seeking to claim superiority in a debate with form, his comment cannot be taken lightly. Seven years ago, when Taniguchi was declared winner of the MoMA design competition, the museum rejected the more dynamic and more experimental forms proposed by Herzog and de Meuron and Bernard Tschumi. In choosing Taniguchi, MoMA seemed to choose a side, if not a winner, in the form debate. (2005: 101–102)

Philip Johnson queried the possibility of a period style under late capitalism in his article for MoMA exhibition on *Deconstructivist Architecture* (curated by Johnson himself and Mark Wigley in 1988). Johnson's position is summed up in the phrase "pluralism reigns" (Johnson: 8). Claims to the universal or global were shunned and hidden at all costs. Johnson wrote:

> [H]owever delicious it would be to declare again a new style, that is not the case today. Deconstructivist architecture is not a new style. We arrogate to its development none of the messianic fervor of the modern movement, none of the exclusivity of that catholic and Calvinist cause. Deconstructivist architecture represents no movement; it is not a creed. It has no 'three rules' of compliance. It is not even 'seven architects.' (8)

If pluralism is all that is possible today, then Riley and MoMA must be particularly forceful if they want to render a style, which is effectively what they have done. But they have not *undone* the preconditions stated by Johnson. MoMA seeks to control an obsolete discourse in the form of its own self-image. They have produced a contemporary architecture in the form of a weak, undeconstructed, or hollowed out modernist minimalism. It checks all the necessary aesthetic boxes but remains empty at the core. It has no heralding sense of the future to come. It is not a beacon of light in the darkness. It has none of modernism's ethic of the future. If the museum admits contemporaneity in adding contemporary galleries to its design, it has not followed through architecturally.

Johnson came near to announcing a paradoxical "antimovement movement" in the act of denouncing the very possibilities of Movement today, which implies a high level of certainty about where we are headed historically. "Movement" is not part of "the contemporary", where here it has been banished to the modern, archaic, or nostalgic, like analogue technology. The museum perpetuates itself and, like some political parties, it may only fully exist within its own imagination. MoMA has power and authority; MoMA *does* contribute to the very creation of the coming paradigm. Its authorial signature is transferred to the architects and enhances their possibility for success. The seven architects in Johnson and Wigley's MoMA exhibition—showcasing Frank Gehry, Daniel Libeskind, Rem Koolhaas, Peter Eisenman, Zaha Hadid, Coop Himmelblau, and Bernard Tschumi—went on to become big stars—the so-called "starchitects"—in the 1990s and 2000s. This was no accident. These architects were united, as John Rajchman has argued, but not through an idea of "deconstruction" (they were not interested in Jacques Derrida), but in a shared anti-postmodernist attitude—one that refuted quotationalist and historicist techniques—which expressed itself through the retrieval of modernist aesthetic tactics, which could then be re-branded as "contemporary" (Rajchman 2003). A curious paradox emerges; the decision to use Taniguchi's design meant a departure from everything these seven architects were trying to do. Taniguchi can be said to be historicist because of his deployment of a version of the Bauhaus, however boutique a vision. Of the seven architects, Koolhaas, Eisenman, and Tschumi were in MoMA's charette, and Tschumi, along with Jacques Herzog and Pierre de Meuron—later to become known for the Tate Modern, London—were the finalists.

Let us turn to the Koolhaas entry, because more than the other designs his proposal concentrated an effort to radically redirect the institution down a different historical path. Unlike the more complacent Taniguchi, Koolhaas did not offer the comfort of continuity. Rather, the OMA's proposal exhibited a concrete enactment of the "tradition of the new" (to use Harold Rosenberg's phrase), as opposed to a mere frame for the new. In 1997, Koolhaas commented on the state of the museum:

> I look at MoMA for the first time as an architect and I'm shocked. Shocked at the difference—I had never really "seen" MoMA, only looked at its contents (or its machinery). The old part of MoMA is shabby; the new part of MoMA [Cesar Pelli's] is tacky. While ingenious, the architectural quality of the 80's extension is dubious: its identity is blurred and compromised, its galleries have no particular qualities, the basement seems conceived as a corporate purgatory. (2004b: 195)[13]

My fundamental interpretation is that the redesign, reconstruction, and expansion is indicative not of a museum whose achievement keeps building, but of a museum in the throes of a singular crisis. It is with this thought that we may turn to the museum that *could have been*. Koolhaas did even make it into MoMA committee's final selection. MoMA can be charged with having used its own safe terms, privileging a reified version of modernism, namely "international style" minimalism, and a whole vocabulary of architecture promoted virtually for

---

[13] The OMA's book, produced as a proposal to the Museum, *M(oMA) Charette: How to Make the Most of the Museum Boom* (1997), which totals 400-pages, is currently unpublished. Muschamp noted: "As much a philosophical critique of the museum as a plan for its physical enlargement, the book deserves wider circulation" (Muschamp 1997). Really it ought to be published. Some of the book's pages are reproduced in the OMA volume *Content* (Taschen 2004), but at a scale difficult to read without a magnifying glass; it is not adequate.

the occasion. When the architects involved in generating ideas for the new architecture offered up alternatives, MoMA seems to have looked the other way, preferring that which represented an aesthetic continuation with the old rather than a break into the new. The Taniguchi building is contemporary in the superficial sense but complacent in its perpetuation of a once-revolutionary, now hegemonic, style. From Koolhaas' architect's statement:

> Theoretically, MoMA is about newness. Newness is ambiguous. It cannot last; it cannot have a tradition ... The splendor and uniqueness of MoMA's history complicates its relationship with the present. The expectation of continuity penalizes what is "other", what does not "fit", or the "merely" contemporary. Beyond its power to intimidate, to set standards, to consecrate, an entire domain of exploration, experimentation has become problematic: its investment in a master narrative and the abundant evidence to support "the line" make certain new shows seem like mere tokenism or simply impossible. What can you challenge in a temple ... In this project, we have interpreted the extension as a single operation that maintains what is good, undoes what is dysfunctional, creates new potentials, and leaves open what is undecidable ... The creation of a single display building—a new MoMA—implies that it can be fully equipped to generate unique conditions for each segment of the collections and any of the exhibitions. It will have to accommodate drastically different scales .... Because .... the new building will contain the entire Museum program, it will have the advantages of bigness. (MoMA Archives, MoMA, New York, NY)

Koolhaas's redesign proposal offers to save the museum only by destroying it first, by "dislodging the present positions", which was the slogan the OMA team worked under for this project (Fig. 3). It is a design premised not on restoration, not on returning to a mythical modernist or Bauhaus set of clean lines, but an embrace of the museum's multiple functions, only one of which is the display of art.

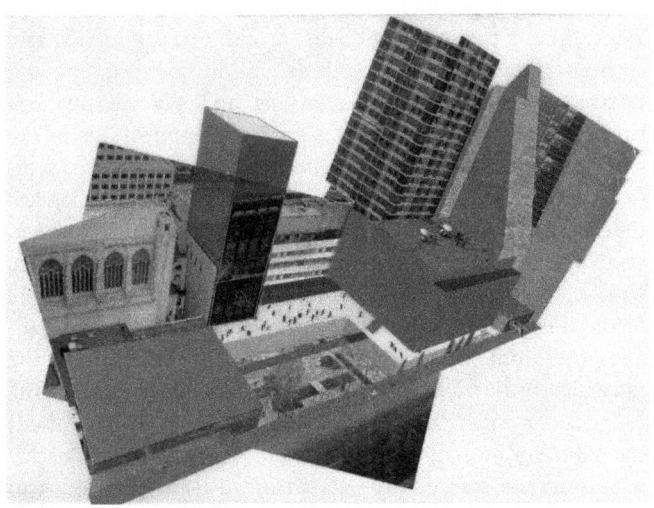

*Figure 3.* Rem Koolhaas and O.M.A., Charrette Submission for The Museum of Modern Art Expansion, New York, NY, 1997. © 2014. Digital image, The Museum of Modern Art, New York/Scala, Florence.

Then-architecture critic for *The New York Times,* Herbert Muschump, noted that the museum has many functions "other than aesthetic contemplation. It sells watches. It throws parties. It courts the media. It makes deals. These functions … could be architecturally expressed" (Muschump 1996). Rising out of Johnson's 1964 wing, Koolhaas positions a seven-storey tower called "MoMA, Inc", which is conceived as holding all the administrative offices, a flatly corporate monument to the big business of contemporary art and the contemporary management of modern art. Koolhaas wanted to bring the museum's current Lowry-paradigm into explicit relation to the body of the museum. It is a critical proposal, in this sense, in trying, as if following the Russian Formalist concept, to "lay bare the conditions of production".

Taniguchi did not produce any alienation effects. Koolhaas was opposed to the idea of making the architecture "disappear", as Taniguchi winningly proposed. The OMA's was a proposal, an experiment, for making the museum show its workings as a part of the globalist machine of production and consumption. Koolhaas was under no illusions that art and culture are manufactured relations and perceptions, not simply objects for display. It signifies an opposition to the new bourgeois or hegemonic "international style". The architect was not interested in deploying architecture to conceal the fact that museums give grace and "soul" to money, power, and violence. To signal his irony, he proposed chandeliers to hang in the main atrium. This final touch is the true opposite of the theoretical and minimalist underpinnings of the Bauhaus tradition, which Koolhaas wanted to finally break the museum *away from*. Had this proposal been accepted, the foundations might have been laid for genuine debate about the nature of museums, the legacies of modernism and architecture in late commodity capitalism. Instead, in contrast to Koolhaas, the museum opted for safe continuity, silencing contemporary contradictions through homage to the past, to nostalgia.

Taniguchi's massive atrium space is homage to a future that may already have been cancelled, a Utopian space far too big for anything the museum currently owns. It is a space that imagines the future as Bigness, an idea that comes out of postwar Minimalism, in which works could not be perceived in their totality and only grasped through duration and in the movement of one's body through space—such as the large architectural and sculptural works of Serra—works which are given central placement in the Guggenheim, Bilbao and at Dia: Beacon in New York. In 2007, however, Serra was given his first retrospective at MoMA (or anywhere)—a show that would have been unthinkable in the pre-Taniguchi MoMA. The museum and Serra are in contemporaneity with one another. Taniguchi's MoMA and Serra are coeval expressions of the limit that MoMA has experienced within the last two decades.

One finds a parallel to this limit in other works of sculpture in this period, such as staple Jeff Koons steel balloon objects or Louise Bourgeois spiders, which are repeatedly installed outside the entrances to the new museums (such as the Mori Art Museum in Tokyo, the Leeum, Samsung Museum of Art in Seoul, and the Tate Modern, to name a few), or pasted into architectural renderings. These artworks have by now long since functioned to present architecture and architects as politically inoffensive, announcing that you have stepped into the smooth safety of globalised consumer space.

The museum in its reconstruction has become not so much a museum as a *palace*, the thing that the very institution of the museum negated historically (in France, after the 1789 revolution). Its campus exceeds that of the immediate and accessible object-filled spaces for the visitor and overflows into the many hundreds of rooms and residential apartments within Pelli's tower on top of the museum and further with an additional tower designed by Jean Nouvel.[14] The introduction of "the contemporary" signals that something has changed. This change signifies a shift in meaning—a defeat, a victory, or entry into enigma. It is the entry of contemporaneity into the museum: a difficult, incomplete, and unmapped condition.

---

[14] Jean Nouvel's 75-story tower (1,050-foot) will rise up against MoMA and into in the sky above it dwarfing Pelli's 1984 tower. The international developer Hines has proposed a mixed facility, with culture and commerce melding high above street level: a hotel, luxury apartments, and three floors for use by the museum, which may act as an extension to the modern and contemporary galleries. It has been conceived of as mutually beneficial for the business of the tower and museum alike; MoMA gets another 40,000 square feet of exhibition space and Hines gains philanthropic prestige—two types of contemporary capital. *New York Times* critic of architecture, Nicholai Ouroussoff, raised a question: "How did a profit-driven developer become more adventurous architecturally than MoMA, which has tended to make cautious choices in recent years?" (Ouroussoff 2007).

The task of the museum is to map the aesthetic response to the condition of the contemporary. But it goes beyond admitting a new style, adding another innovation or another generation to the collection, or hailing a hitherto unappreciated medium. "The contemporary" represents the arrival of the continuous historical critique of ourselves, in Foucauldian terms—of who we are. This category is the perpetual attempt to answer the question set up by Kant in "What is Enlightenment?": What difference does today introduce with respect to yesterday?

The deployment of "the contemporary" therefore represents a final institutional reconfiguring, if belatedly. It is best understood as the emergence into the conditions that arrive when societies become critical of modernity, but still seem to lack a viable alternative to modernity. In this time (unlike in postmodernism, which still held an essential attitude, however critical, towards modernism), neither continental Europe nor North America are the necessary central co-ordinates of the most consequential artistic production. That the museum is enamoured still of Euro- and American-centricity is partly because of historical inheritance, but that is not an excuse for a lack of risk in which, or whose, contemporaneity the museum decides to exhibit.

In addition, or as a consequence of these changes, the role of this museum has undergone a change in the early twenty-first century. Its unquestioned authority has waned (despite the success of "MoMA" as a brand, one that in the Museum Design Store on 53$^{rd}$ Street can be attached to any piece of design imaginable). This retraction of power finds a parallel loss of power in the city of New York itself, which was the city of modernity par excellence.

The contemporary is not a neutral zone. It is not what Roland Barthes called a "zero degree" or what Alfred H. Barr thought was "supine neutrality". The contemporary is not a value-free zone precisely because of the cultural work of valuation and appraisal performed by ideological apparatuses such as MoMA. To riff on Jameson's insight, as "modernism" came to be held as the aesthetic and intellectual response to an incomplete modernisation, so too can Contemporary Art now be reconceived (its task, that is) as the aesthetic response to incomplete contemporaneity.

MoMA's atrium and the large Contemporary Galleries signify the new centrality of 3D: sculpture, installation, and object are privileged. We are not confronted with a proliferation of walls for hanging flat pictures, but gigantic spaces in which to place or suspend things. To scan the Modernist Galleries today for the predecessor to our paradigm-of-no-paradigm is to arrive not at Picasso's *Les Demoiselles d'Avignon*, which still had gravitas in the 1984 Pelli redesign of the museum, but at Duchamp's *readymades* and his large glass works. Dada is the financial-architectural Unconscious of the Taniguchi redesign.

MoMA has admitted contemporaneity and the contemporary—meaning Bigness and the historical legacy of Dada—into its very shape, size, and being. But the museum is not meeting this challenge. It may be a problem within the ontology and conception of art itself today—a reasoning towards which Arthur Danto would probably be sympathetic. Art may not be able to perform its function with the subject of today, who may have mutated in another direction—maybe towards the archive or the screen.

The new museums (and MoMA is no exception here) are deployed and redeployed to economic ends. Globalism, as the ideology of globalisation, is commerce-driven development with the World Trade Organisation (founded in 1995) at its centre.[15] Luxuriously architectural museums of the contemporary are deployed as signs of the public success of new countries and of cities being swept up into the world picture of simultaneous asynchronicity. For John Ralston Saul, the historic originality of globalism lay in its acceptance of commerce or "the reconceptualisation of civilisation through economics" (115) as the key shaping force for human events; the

---

[15] The WTO became a collective cultural symbol of the excesses of the system by 1999, most notably in the Seattle protests.

past, Saul argued, had relied on politics and armies (16). The high visibility of politics and armies is what we begin to witness once more when globalism enters into shutdown and collapse; the museums, as in 2002 (especially in the US), empty out and lay off staff, and sometimes even reduce lighting, due to shrinking tourist numbers.

The point that must be stressed is that the condition of "the contemporary" as distinct from the modern and the postmodern, albeit with signs of inheritance from both of those paradigms, is not just an idea that critics and theorists bring to the museum and apply coldly from the outside. On the contrary, it comes from above; it is an idea signalled by the new museum itself, by its own hot act of reconstruction. Since MoMA's new building demonstrates the inclusion of official Contemporary Art in the collection, the contemporary has become a part of its standing as much as a part of its reading of modernity; "the contemporary" signifies the long historical decline of modernity's confidence, conceptual and Hegelian relevance. One hopes that the revelation of the uses of the discourse at this museum may be illuminating for those who wish to undermine the activities of what has been justly called by Michael Kimmelman the "corporate headquarters of modernism" (35).

The big reconstruction is an attempt by the museum to "territorialise" the contemporary, but it is a necessarily incomplete territorialisation. MoMA in its new form is a museum readied for contemporaneity, poised for it, which, at this particular institution, may indeed be waiting for an arrival that may never come.

# 04: Complacencies of the New Architecture

> It is no wonder the majority of architects avoid the political implications of their work. They believe themselves to be creators, or innovators, when in actuality they are nothing more nor less than the executors of a physical and social order designed by those institutions presently holding political authority and power.
> 
> Lebbeus Woods

The narrative of architecture raises the critique of "the contemporary" paradigm to a whole new level. One of the suggestions of this book is that unlike the modern and the postmodern, "the contemporary" is without a project. A distinction must be drawn here between a critical project that the contemporary lacks and the default "project" that constitutes the ideology of the contemporary that might simply be boiled down to *growth*, which is of course capitalism's necessity. So it is not altogether without a project, but the project of which it is a part is that of the commodity's territorialisation of untried grounds, whether these are national, aesthetic, or the market. In architecture and museums, growth, expansion, addition, mutation, bigness, and extension (all fundamentally phallic, yes) are characteristics of the "contemporary" ethos before the money crash, but also after it when élitism continued to soar, with a dialectic of "monopolise further or risk obsolescence".

The pressures and conditions to renew and expand on contemporist discourse are instructive, especially at the intersections of built space. More has been invested in the construction of "the contemporary" in the Australian context within the last two decades than ever before. The Museum of Contemporary Art in Sydney received a series of combined private donations for an expansion that allowed the museum, which had desired a new building since its founding in 1991, to grow its floor-space and express its mission in an architectural statement.[1] The MCA's new wing is hardly on the scale of Dubai (as will be discussed later)—to take today's arguably most outstanding example of expansive excess, where, before the money crash of 2008, billion dollar mega-projects were announced on a near weekly basis—but the announcement is symptomatic for our purposes, signalling that "contemporary" is valuable in itself, and remains open to investment; to this extent, it is commercially and culturally meaningful in both the government and private sectors from which the funding came. All this time, "contemporary" remained a sincere paradigm, exercising incredible flexibility to stay the same while all around it was irreversibly altered, with no move to a "post-contemporary" of any kind on the horizon.

The MCA was among the first museums anywhere to mix the once contradictory meanings of "museum" and "contemporary", a binary that has long since been effaced. The new MCA had several false starts in this last decade before the project gained traction and was built. In 2007, the museum's director Elizabeth Ann MacGregor hoped that the new building would have the effect that Jeff Koons's oversized, flower-bed sculpture *Puppy* (which eventually found its home in Bilbao,

---

[1] MCA chairman David Coe and MCA Foundation chairman Simon Mordant each gave starting sums of five million dollars, in the hope that other donors would follow (*The Australian*, August 23, 2007)—they did. It was also an opportunity for this museum to grow its ideological reach, nationalistically, which it did by rebranding itself as the MCA, Australia as opposed to the MCA, Sydney.

Spain) had for the museum in 1999 when it graced the front lawn: "What *Puppy* did for us was say contemporary ... That's what the extension will do. So while I'm going on about respecting the heritage, what we really want is for people to go: 'That's a contemporary building!'" (Westwood 2007).

What MacGregor desired was to construct an irresolute connection between the contemporary and the new building. The MCA originally opened in the Maritime Services Board building, a pseudo-art deco work of architecture that has been described as "a Stalinist, fascist building" and also, contrarily, as an unthreatening "dull monolith" (Smith 2001: 29). All this time, the museum has not possessed adequate space to hang a permanent display of the contemporary art that it collects— that is, to act as a *museum* rather than a gallery. For a while it seemed that the old MSB building would be bulldozed to make way for a purpose-built work taking advantage of the whole site. Indeed, in 2001 Terry Smith supported such a move on the condition that its replacement was "of Utzon's [of Sydney Opera House fame] order of imaginative invention, only if it possessed the qualities of art to come" (2001: 29). Smith suggested Frank Gehry's massive Guggenheim Museum proposal for downtown Manhattan (later cancelled by the events of 9/11) as a model of inspiration.

In the MCA's redesign, Sam Marshall chose to extend the old building rather than demolish it. The new MCA's exterior has been widely named "cubistic" which would seem to contain some reference, however oblique, to high modernism (although historical Czech cubist architecture, the most developed cubism in architecture, was of a very different order). The modernist critic Owen Hatherlay calls this kind of venture "pseudomodernism", a style that sees "postmodernism's incorporation of a modernist formal language" and a "lack of deliberate architectural-historical references and jokes" (Hatherlay 2010: xx). This is not really modernism as it lacks aggression, but it is not postmodern either as there are no jokes or critiques of the past. The new building offers a partial reminting of modernist tendency, a lite brutalism: neutralised, inoffensive, and unchallenging.

The boldly capitalised word "Contemporary" is emblazoned, without irony, on the outside of the new wing. It is significant that the term can be used meaningfully, without seeming used up, overfull, clichéd, and that it inspires curiosity (strollers at the Quay are solicited to feel that the category includes or invites them) but not quizzicality (alienation, a true modernist thematic, is presumably bad for business). It is positioned on the building's exterior across a right angle, and from the front view of the building the "temporary" part of the word stands out. This framing, intentionally or not, registers both the question of temporality and the ambiguities and doubt in and around the "contemporary" ethos. Not unlike the remake of New York's MoMA, the museum registers its own hesitations to define the contemporary even as it paradoxically generates definition, language, and context for it via presentation, collection, authorisation, groupings of works, and canonisation, etc. Underscoring the feeling that the time is out of joint, the MCA relaunched with the theme of time itself—*Volume One: Marking Time.*

MacGregor did not campaign for a signifier of the modern or the postmodern; something definitively new is occurring in this kind of desire that might be explained with reference to what architects have been calling the "Bilbao effect" for reasons that have to do with Frank Gehry's architectural megasuccess in Bilbao at the end of the 1990s. In a word, architecture (which has always been understood as the closest art to commerce) becomes a sort of extension to the marketing and branding of place (not unlike the original effect of Utzon's Sydney Opera House across the Quay in the 1970s). In driving gentrification and the concentration of capital, the seductive deployment of architecture becomes a political project for changing the city fabric itself—creating a dot on the map, driving metropolitan expansion. The perceived need for this commodity "the contemporary" is in part due to the pressure to be a global city, which Sydney aspires towards, seeing itself as requiring a comparable institution to Taniguchi's MoMA and the widely celebrated Tate Modern. The MCA remains a different kind of institution, of course, critically positioned partly because of its marginality. Nonetheless, there is a structure of competitiveness to the contemporary; a closeness, undoubtedly, to the heart of capitalism, if such a bio-morphism (which implies a warm and feeling subject) is permissible in describing the cold and reified processes of capital. There is also a perceived global map of museums that is imagined to be so in tune with capitalism that a city is able to buy or speculate on its position through architecture alone, nowhere more evident than in Abu Dhabi's planned concentration of European and American museum and university franchises. MacGregor supported the development model that the Tate used in the year 2000 of a mix of retail, museum, and education—the open secret of blurring commerce and culture that we may take on board as a sign that contemporaneity is at work.

Shifting regions dramatically to Riga, Latvia, a major Museum of Contemporary Art planned for the banks of the Dalthuva, designed by Rem Koolhaas, has been put on hold by the European money crisis. The proposal itself signals a significant shift; accordingly, I will sketch a view of this development as it was before cancellation. The British Council has maintained a role of promoting small, artist-run activities in the advancement, and construction, of the contemporary in the Baltic States, as have the Soros Centres throughout Eastern Europe. Latvia (which gained independence in 1991) has not had an MCA to its name, or even a museum devoted solely to modern art.[2] For the former Second World of Europe,

---

[2] It is interesting to note that in contradistinction, Vilnius, the capital of Lithuania—Latvia's economically less well-off neighbour—invested in a Contemporary Art Center, or CAC, almost immediately after gaining independence in 1992, becoming one of the largest in all of post-Soviet Europe. Since October 2004, the CAC has produced its own show for commercial Lithuanian television (http://www.cac.lt/tv) that manifests the CAC's commitment to contemporaneity, as a kind of formal homage to the extreme state of being in the present. The show's slogan is, "every episode is a pilot, and every program is the final episode". It is described thus: "An amorphous group of social misfits and cultural outcasts are handed the reins of a fledgling television program. Not having any experience in making television,

"the contemporary" arrives as a kind of shining beacon of post-Communist hope, a true sign of the integration of the Baltic States, among others, into the Western capitalism they have sought for a long time. (The capitalism they have now achieved is of course part of a much later capitalism than the North American version to which they originally aspired as part of the escape plan from Soviet totalitarianism.) The museum would stand alongside the sombre, black, windowless Museum of the Soviet Occupation of Latvia 1940-91, in the same city, as a contrast and message: to be contemporary is to be finally beyond the Cold War, to be in (a kind of) freedom, and even more so, to be part of the "Blue Europe" that is the European Union, and a strong sign of success through conformity especially for the once-comparatively impoverished Eastern Bloc countries.[3] Indeed, the non-contemporaneity of the Soviet example of modernity goes beyond the static obser-

---

they decide to re-invent the medium. CAC/TV is a time-slot for imagining alternate realities." It is also interesting to note that the Guggenheim Foundation and the city of Vilnius are in discussion about developing a Guggenheim alongside the Nevis, and that the media have been fed an artist's impression of the new building designed by Zaha Hadid.

[3] The term Blue Europe, sometimes written "Blueurope", was used in a derogatory fashion by the Office for Metropolitan Architecture (OMA/AMO) in its commission by the EU to address Europe's "iconographic deficit", its perceived vagueness or shapelessness, within global politics and the global economy—that is, to find a way to better articulate the EU as a "project" (DeGraaf and Koolhaas 2004g: 388). Drastically simplifying, the OMA/AMO's concept was developed around the rejection of the blue flag currently recognised, according to the project's designers, as the sign of unwanted homogeneity. The office proposed a "barcode" flag instead: "Europe shown as the sum of the cultural identities of its current and future members. Whereas the number of stars on the current EU flag is fixed, the barcode can accommodate newcomers" (Koolhaas 2004g: 384). The success or failure of this kind of project, which involves no architecture or policy change, relies on the power of image and imagined communities (in Benedict Anderson's heavily politicised sense) to communicate its point.

vation that there is no "actually existing socialism" in that country today, or the former bloc itself, and the question of any possible alternative to capitalist contemporaneity is quietly sidelined along with it.

There is something quietly authoritarian in the ubiquity of "the contemporary" and the slogan's apparent self-identity with global capitalism's expansionist mode. We could also look, in an example from the Czech Republic, to Prague's appropriation of Gehry's architecture in the so-called Dancing Building along the Charles River: a small but significant work for its ideological content. Gehry's aesthetic of free-flowing expressionism became a sign of post-Communist integration into the world of global capitalism; in the new global situation, even buildings—or especially buildings—are not static, necessarily permanent structures. There is a discourse of liberation embedded within the deployment of "the contemporary" which has become identified with Western freedom in the forms of profit, consumption, and choice. Contemporaneity underwent a boom with the fall of Eastern European Communism and the emergence of a more complete global capitalism. It is a deployment of the term the default economic content of which is capitalist, its political content is neo-liberal (or possibly neo-fascist?), and its tacit cultural acceptance is global.

## COGNITIVE MAPPING

In framing architectural contemporaneity's difference from high modernism and postmodernism, I will use the unique and relatively under-discussed place that the late modern architect Minoru Yamasaki (1912-1986) has come to occupy within questions of contemporaneity—in particular, Yamasaki's Utopian housing scheme Pruitt-Igoe of the 1950s, which underwent planned demolition in the early 1970s, and the architect's equally ambitious financial pseudo-Utopia the Manhattan World Trade Center, completed in the early 1970s and destroyed in the 9/11 shock attack in 2001. In my historical examples using Yamasaki, we see architecture functioning within trajectories of Utopian possibility, disappointment, and aftermath. In each subsequent analysis—the Freedom Tower (renamed as completion was approached in an apparent attempt to neutralize discussion), the China Central Television headquarters in Beijing (CCTV), the massive deployment of architecture in Dubai and Abu Dhabi, and, among others, the uncertain status of the United Nations headquarters—I argue that ultimately we see contemporaneity functioning as an aggressive, reflexive modernism, without modernity's once-strong ethic of the future.

My strategically selected examples are works that exemplify certain conditions of "the contemporary". In these we see various instances of architecture as a function of nostalgia (US), power (China), wealth (UAE), and uncertainty (United Nations). In the emerging—necessarily fragmentary—picture that accrues of these developments, far from the globalising fantasy of the decline of nation-states, are aggressive post-international and post-ethical projects that do not assimilate to the well-trodden categories of modernity and postmodernity. We see something else: modernity without Utopia—a modernity that has forfeited its relationship to the future, and a modernity characterised by an enigma that is no longer grasped as a problem to be solved. The architect George Katodrytis provides a characterisation of that inevitable, and irresistible, part of the architectural wing of the contemporaneity discussion that is Dubai:

> Dubai is a prototype of the new post-global city, which creates appetites rather than solves problems ... If Rome was the 'Eternal City' and New York's Manhattan the apotheosis of twentieth-century congested urbanism, then Dubai may be considered the emerging prototype for the 21st century: prosthetic and nomadic oases presented as isolated cities that extend out over the land and the sea. (Katodrytis 2005)

Such celebratory accounts of vast consumption centred around luxury and cultural élitism, such as those offered by

Katodrytis, are no doubt great for the Gulf's developers and for business (Davis 2006: 50). I will come back to the example of Dubai later in this chapter. The following seeks to show how the paradigm of contemporaneity is different from modernity and postmodernity. We saw how "the contemporary" functions as a vacuous term awaiting content, a term so open and flexible as to be able to accommodate virtually anything. Unlike the modern and the postmodern, the contemporary was revealed as non-programmatic; it was enigmatic (in Perniola's sense). We also saw how the enigma of the contemporary has been used by the Museum of Modern Art—an institution that was once focused exclusively on defining the modern and bringing it to a public that awaited arrivals from future worlds. Today, the contemporary, as the replacement ideology of the modern and postmodern descriptors of the present moment, functions as an *aporia*—the Greek meaning of which is an "unpassable path". In other words, we do not expect to go beyond "the contemporary", and hardly expect the MoMA, a diffused institution living inside its own historical self-image, to be able to do so. The contemporary has become an inconsistent deployment that is frequently negative and positive at the same time: poison *and* antidote (in the familiar Derridean or deconstructionist example), hegemonic *and* critical of the system. As I will emphasise, Rem Koolhaas is the best example of the architect of contemporaneity; he lives this contradiction as an explicit part of his work, with the critical writings that point to a new vision of history on the one hand, and the construction of a building in support of twenty-first century totalitarian capitalism on the other.

The narrative of architecture is one that has been highly constructed in the critical theory of modernism and postmodernism, and in many instances has become the very centre of the debate about new times—a different paradigm, a new wave, an emergent episteme. It is perhaps the most obvious cultural site to turn to in seeking the indicative, consequential, most visible, as well as curiously *slowest* deployments of "the contemporary". (Architecture, unlike the other arts, takes an average of five years of execution, meaning that, by completion time, a work is often outmoded or practically non-contemporary.) Architecture is the most visible art in the sense that we can see both the spatial expression, construction, and reproduction of the social and financial system itself in real built developments, and the often highly celebrated developments repeated again and again in the mass media, where they take on new functions and values within that system (which is mostly global capitalism). Terry Smith in *The Architecture of Aftermath* uses the neologism "iconomy" to exemplify this condition. Visual and spatial affect-based architecture plans ahead, at least in part, for existence within the iconomy, and can be seen early on in the example of Jorn Utzon's Sydney Opera House, and more recently—more effectively—in Frank Gehry's Guggenheim Museum in Bilbao, arguably "*the* symbol of ascension of the symbolic to the level of major economic lever and driver in a world order that was everywhere understood as animated by spectacularity" (Smith 2006b: 23). Such works are dramatically conscious of their own spectacle, have large public force, spawn a lot of commentary, and therefore loom large in the imagination of mass consciousness and the imagination of "architecture". The quality of individual design presides over the sheer quantity of mass-produced architecture: the sites where most people work and reside, the generic cities that lie behind all episodes of the spectacular. Smith defines the iconomy thus:

> While singular in its configuration, it [the iconomy] is also, and primarily, a precipitator of mobility—its own reproducibility, and that of its viewers. This type of iconic image is a generator of a variety of values: it may pleasure the eye, arouse the flesh, or stimulate the mind. With the current globalised state of capital, however, it does these things in order to produce economic value. Not, however, simply as money—although that is a major measure of how its capacity stands to other economic agents—but as itself: an iconotype spins off countless images of itself ... Further, it promotes the iconomy itself, the entire economy of which it is part. (2006b: 22–23)

The debate about contemporaneity has largely come out of issues relating directly to architecture—the built environment, what Henri Lefebvre called the "production of space" in the book by that name, and (adapting Althusser's phrase) what we might call the "reproduction of the conditions of the production of space". The debate about modernity began with the topic of architecture. Indeed, new cultural paradigms, reflective of the undercurrent of the history of capital itself, find their earliest signs within this disciplinary force field. Very early indications of the shift to modernity and modern times conventionally draw on examples that relate to architecture and the use of city space. For instance, we may think of the storming of the Bastille in 1789, which opens one of the vast new eras of enlightenment history. Equally, the occupation of the Louvre and its cultural repurposing as a museum is another instance of the same moment. The French example is useful in this instance, to which we may add Eugene Haussmann's development of Paris' immense boulevards in the late 1850s and 1860s (under imperial mandate of Napoleon III), which signified the new conception of the city and of city and communal space with "new roads as arteries in an urban circulatory system" (Berman 1988: 150) that sought to unify the congested and isolated medieval city beneath, creating new vistas of space for collective movement which made possible, and reflected, the new modern lifestyle articulated by Baudelaire, and others. Engineering marvels, early instances of High Tech, added to the use of building as a sign and deployment of power and modernity for its own sake. For instance, take the example of "Eiffel's great tower" in the late 1880s (Smith 2006b: 123).[4] These images, which are commonplace today,

---

[4] Smith, in his review of architecture in the immediate before and after of 9/11, uses the term "engineering featurism" to describe those works of architecture in the contemporary that foreground sophisticated and often kinetic aspects over other possible stylistic, social, or political contents; this is best exemplified in the works of Santiago Calatrava. Engineering featurism is one of four "main trajectories within advanced architecture of the West". The other trajectories are, open-form spectacle (Frank Gehry), past-modern quotation (Richard

were revolutionary in their eighteenth and nineteenth century contexts. They may be becoming relevant again in light of the current modernities in China where whole sections of Beijing have been cleared out, rebuilt, and the masses relocated in new high rises. The city was decked out with extra-large architectural icons parachuted in by European and American architects at the opportunistic moment of the artificial time cycle that is the Olympic Games.

The revisioning of entire cities is indeed part of the modernist attitude. Le Corbusier did not have his vision for the future of Paris realised, but he envisioned collective transformation in terms of stamping out whole sections of the existing place and its replacement with "radiant cities" or gleaming towers in new parks. Architecture, many commentators on modernity have argued, provides the sharpest insight into, in Marx's terms, the fact that "Men [sic] make their own history, but not spontaneously, under conditions they have chosen for themselves; rather on terms immediately existing, given and handed down to them" (287). This is true both in relation to the projects of the architect's visions and the collectives or masses who had no say in matters of great architectural shift or the mutation of cities. Those masses experienced modernity as an unstoppable top-down force, as many in China have recently. Contemporary modernisation in China offers a strong argument for the Jamesonian notion, via Freud, of a "return of the repressed" (Jameson 2002: 7) of modernity itself in the aftermath of the postmodern moment; the displacement of people from their homes in Beijing to make way for "progress"; in contradiction to the idea of progress, the "tangible cases of forced eviction and the demolition of residential areas without payment or any (or adequate) compensation" (Birkholz 2006: 127) speaks volumes about the repetition of the kind of architectural modernity Europe witnessed in the nineteenth-century and early to mid-twentieth. This is to say nothing of the virtual slave labour camps (or whole provision-

---

Meier), and "grounding the contradictions" (Daniel Libeskind) (2007: 123).

al sleeper cities) erected in the perimeters of the new global construction sites, in Singapore, Dubai, etc. The long global historical narrative of modernity appears to have shifted from Western Europe to North America, and now from North America to the dramatically different situations of Asia, the Middle East, and, to some extent, post-Soviet Eastern Europe. They have one commonality: an élite of global architects or "star architects" (who, like their buildings, also function as images within the iconomy) flitting from place to place and competition to competition, all surfing the variously chaotic and celebratory movements of the extra-large capital that makes the bigness of current-age architecture possible.

The debate about postmodernity was also kick-started by a discussion in architecture. Again, the most visible instances of the crucial cultural changes at hand in the mid to late twentieth-century were *seen* in the phenomenon of buildings and the mutations within the city brought about by new formal structures, which were sometimes veritable cities in their own right—mega-structures that threatened to displace our sense of the otherwise knowable city that had been made possible by technologies of the steel-frame, elevator, escalator, and air-conditioner. The architecture of the increasingly megalithic shopping malls (successors to the arcades analysed by Walter Benjamin in *The Arcades Project*), hotels, and theme parks the size of Manhattan and larger, indicated that shifts were again at hand. This is one version of the postmodern. Another can be seen in the explicit rejection of the whole tradition of modernist design, and belief in unbridled progress and development. The project of modernity was cast under monumental suspicion. Henceforth, the sense of living within modernity will no longer be that of living within a project, but rather one of competing private pseudo-Utopias—at the levels of individual building, residence, and city—and violently opposed worldviews roughly corresponding to the political revival of the nation-state. Henceforth, we are living in enigmatic times, which are post-ethical, vastly non- or even anti-programmatic, and post-co-operational in nature (which can be seen in the norm of neo-liberal competition-based architecture projects).

In the following, provisional samples are offered of the scene of architecture through the lens of projects that are of particular significance for their apparent break with both the attitude of the modern and that of the postmodern. This unique constellation is not representative of all that is going on in the architecture of "the contemporary". In a final note, upon the mission of political architecture today, I will draw upon the late Venezuelan President Hugo Chavez' call to relocate the United Nations headquarters—that now very faint idea of a post-war Utopian solution to the ongoing crisis of global technological war and increasing radically uneven development. These specific examples of violent monumental heroism might provisionally be termed the *post-international* style, with reference to Philip Johnson and Henry-Russell Hitchcock's 1997 book (*The International Style*) written on the occasion of the Museum of Modern Art's exhibition of 1932, which was inspired by the much earlier International Gothic.

All the developments arisen since the once-final, fatal-seeming postmodern condition that was articulated by Lyotard and Jameson in critical theory, and Charles Jencks and Robert Venturi (among others) in architecture are not mapped here. That task is too great for this context, and at any rate, the act of interpretation at this time of apparent immense transition is more crucial than quantitative almanacs. The genre of the almanac—in this case, devoted to architecture— has seen its own revival recently in Dubai (the book *Al Manakh* was a collaboration by AMO/Archis/C-lab). The almanac form itself indicates the unmanageable quantity of projects in Dubai (and much of the UAE), which can henceforth only be numbered at this extraordinary time of development. The almanac offers an accumulation of data, statistics, and information, rather than judgment or interpretation.

The theoretical pictures of Venturi et al. are now recast as an almost singular moment in time—a blip in aesthetic history, but a significant one, like Italian futurism. In addition to specific examples of that most traditional definition of architecture as the individual building and provision of shelter, I will trace out the careers of two architects of especial importance for our understanding of contemporaneity: Rem Koolhaas (already mentioned) and the late Lebbeus Woods. Vastly different in style, intent, and philosophic approach to their discipline, both architects find meaning in architecture only where the phenomenon intersects with crisis. Both gained recognition through writing; a point I want to emphasise. Each of their major works are attempts to map out a new aspect of the broader crisis of modernist history, which is frankly unthinkable without architecture—a history made by people of superior technological capabilities merging with mobilisations of capital and labour markets on a scale unseen in modern Western history. One need only read Koolhaas' manifestoes on Manhattanism, on Bigness, on the Generic City, and on Junkspace to see a thoroughgoing attempt to think *past* the postmodern moment of Venturi, Jencks, Peter Blake, and others. Both Koolhaas and Woods found ways to turn the crisis of modern history into a crisis of architecture itself.

The different practices of Koolhaas and Woods are examined as practices of architects who have tried to invigorate what might be called an effective culture of *scripting* around architecture, forcing us into awareness of the dominant already-loaded narratives of form, function, and development within architectural practice. These architects, in their different ways, offer a call to interdisciplinary action focused not on building, but on a creative rethinking of what architecture might yet be. They offer projects, however potentially irrational, that are directed outside of the merely contemporaneous, by imagining a future different from the present.

Koolhaas, known equally for his buildings as for his writings, epitomises the ultimate figure of Perniola's enigma, which I have suggested offers a contradictory image for the contemporary. Koolhaas' career and practice is split across incompatible worldviews that extend from the critical turn of his publications and the complacency of his built works, which, admittedly, contribute to a world that is better integrated, sometimes remarkably, into the system of contemporary capital. In Woods, something else entirely is demonstrated. Woods was not a "master builder"—he did construct a few monumental sculptures, but did not effectively build anything that completely qualified as architecture in any conventional sense—but performed as a visionary for the contemporary condition akin to that Italian master of drawn architecture, Giovanni Piranesi—the eighteenth-century illustrator of the fictitious but nonetheless deftly diagnostic *Carceri d'Invenzione*, or "prisons".

What we are dealing with here in the guise of "architecture" is in fact a historical moment that threatens the usefulness of the paradigms of the modern and the postmodern. This chapter is perhaps the most eclectic in the examples it chooses. It is best grasped as what Jameson (adapting the insights of the urban planner Kevin Lynch's book *The Image of the City*) once called a cognitive map of the present, in which "the incapacity to map socially is as crippling to political experience as the analogous incapacity to map spatially is for urban experience" (Jameson 2000b: 283). For Jameson, the construction of such maps was a potentially radical act because it worked explicitly against the fragmentations of the system experienced in the windless ahistorical present: the place in which we live out our lives.

## Utopia and Modernist Failure

Utopia held a central place within the architectural discussion of modernity, and while its concept was enjoyably and critically deconstructed within the postmodern, it remains an unavoidable concern in any analysis of the large projects of today that are driven by complex desires for national triumph and a better world "for some", and the reciprocal impoverishment of the many. The failure of the drive for Utopia is a precondition for the contemporary loss of belief in the future as something we can be committed to in a concrete sense. It must be remembered, however, that there are varieties of the Utopian. In the theorisation of Utopia in critical theory, at least two paths of development are discernible. On the one hand there is the Utopian plan, program, or project, identified by Jameson (among others) as a sweeping design centred around an act of "realisation" that claims to solve and negate a social and political situation, in favour of an actually built and better one. On the other hand, we find what Jameson calls the "Utopian impulse" (2005), which is a markedly different affair, having to do not with building a brand new society or revolution, but with a displaced, striving desire or "wish" to be something else under historical limitations. The impulse offers a hint at a different future or unresolved present, an idea Jameson borrows from Ernst Bloch, and is not a conscious Utopian "project" (Jameson 2005: 6–8). The first might be more generally identified with modernism and the second with the postmodernist, fragmenting globalising city, and its driving force of the iconic building, gentrification, and the Bilbao-effect. The aftermath of the modern and the postmodern—our paradigm-of-no-paradigm (in Hal Foster's terms)—celebrates the individual building to the point of a commodity fetish (in the Frankfurt School sense): the unconscious need to revolutionise our generic cities and our physical and collective ways of living and inter-depending on each other. The icon is also a simplistic construction of place, that other major commodity of the contemporary age, where identity is forged out of chaos and ruin.

Of the arts, architecture does not function without a concept of progress, which my example will link to Utopian and modernist discourse. Architecture may indeed be the strongest site of imagining the future (and of trying to develop a committed politics in relation to it), because the discipline of building, the raw material of construction, and the consequent unavoidable configurations of social space, are always focused on the world to come. In the narrative of development of residential towers, this is seen as the possibility of a better, more efficient, more glamorous, existence (with better views and better urban locations).[5] Yamasaki's career is re-

---

[5] The modernist vision has been turned upside down in real architec-

vealing in this context because of the curious dialogue between Utopia and dystopia we may read into two of his major works: Pruitt-Igoe in St. Louis (1951-1972), and the World Trade Centre in New York (1972-2001). These works, either ambitious modernist plans or projects (vastly different from each other in terms of intentions) have both witnessed a profound reversal of their initial Utopianism, and in turn have problematised the meta-narrative of progress itself. Both works have become famous twice. First, for their individuality and originality, as late modern projects that were future-oriented, collective, and daring in scale; second, for the demolition or outright destruction of the very same works, for vastly different reasons.

Yamasaki's Pruitt-Igoe project in St. Louis, Missouri was a recognised disaster only a few years after its completion. This was an unfortunate fate for one of the many optimistic designs for mass housing of economically disadvantaged populations after the Second World War. When the plan was finished in 1956 it was hailed as a great advance and even took home an award from the American Institute of Architects. But, in 1972, it became a symbol of the separation of plan and Utopia in architecture. There was evidence of disrepair, vandalism, and crime, and people who could afford to do so began moving out; most were forced to stay (see Hoffman). The five million dollars the Housing Authority spent to improve it did not really help; it was not nearly enough money, even then. With demolition, "progress" came to mean—in the well-known reversal—demolition, not construction.[6] The televised

---

tural projects that deployed the highest principles of Corbusian modernity. It has also been wonderfully dramatised as a "dystopia" in fiction—for example, J. G. Ballard's novel *High-Rise* is a narrative with a building at the centre which provides the means or possibility for the descent of young professionals into barbarism and the social disintegration of the luxury tower they have collectively, initially enthusiastically purchased.

[6] Footage of the demolition can be seen in slow-motion to the music of Philip Glass in the 1983 film *Koyaanisqatsi: Life Out of Balance,* directed by Godfrey Reggio.

event of demolition was given iconic status by Charles Jencks: "Modern architecture died in St Louis, Missouri on July 15, 1972 at 3:32pm (or thereabouts) when the infamous Pruitt-Igoe scheme, or rather several of its slab blocks, were given the final *coup de grace* by dynamite" (9). Three of the buildings were demolished and, the following year, all thirty-three of the flat-topped apartment blocks were razed. Looking at photographic stills of the event, today's viewer may discern eerie retrospective overtones of the later spectacle of annihilation—the same architect's very different achievement crashing this time to the streets of Manhattan on 11 September, 2001. This was of course a destruction conducted by quite different parties for quite different reasons on a rather different kind of tower. (That story will not be retold here.)

In Pruitt-Igoe, Utopian planning became slum construction. The plan's demolition has been, for over thirty years now, the example of the failure of modernist Utopian planning in architecture. (Countless other examples could be drawn from Eastern Europe where the mode was favoured by the Soviets, especially where such housing towers have not been torn down.) It is not a closed discussion. For years, at least since Jencks presented his argument in *The Language of Post-Modern Architecture*, this moment has been deployed in articles, student lectures on modern architecture, and textbooks as *the* defining moment of the *death* of modern architecture. A more nuanced reading of Pruitt-Igoe would remind readers that it was the death of a certain phase of post-war modern, and can hardly stand up to the example of modernist development in Asia and the UAE: places that might be redefined as the homes of the global afterlife of modernism. The Pruitt-Igoe moment continues to loom large within the imagination of architects and non-architects alike. The development is notable for its continued connection of modernism as a project that believed in a relationship to the future: an ethical modernism. The project was designed to create community through design and resolve mass poverty. Yamasaki combined open horizontal "galleries" on every third floor with "skip-stop" lifts—elevators that stopped only at gallery floors and that required residents to go up or down stairs to get to their apartments—with the intention of community construction (an anti-alienation device). Design was intended to perform forced encounters between residents going about their lives. But it was not long before these innovative experiments were widely known nuisances and danger zones (Hoffman). In addition, to save funds and house more people, services such as gyms, a green grocer, and playgrounds were removed from the plan, with the sole remaining artefact a community centre (which merely kept the Housing Authority rent collectors).

The most visible Utopian element of Pruitt-Igoe lies in its ideological association with the classical modernist vision, which had to do with abstract space and universal geometries, as opposed to the radical specificity of place (Venturian "context"), the identity and complexity of population, and situated need. The teleological belief held that the modernist aesthetic, in Jameson's words, "proceeded triumphalistically from the new to the newest" (2002: 1). The ever-enlarging secular and technological enlightenment suggested "progress toward a perfected world was inevitable, making the past obsolete" (Birmingham). For Yamasaki, the teleology of Pruitt-Igoe was meant to distil down into the very bodies of its inhabitants. As Jencks says: "[I]ts Purist style, its clean, salubrious hospital metaphor, was meant to instil, by good example, corresponding virtues in the inhabitants ... intelligent planning of abstract space was to promote healthy behaviour" (9). But all this occurred within the structure of class society, so it is not necessarily tenable to compare the highest ideals of architectural modernity with Pruitt-Igoe, which, as a state adaptation of such ideals, meant poorer quality materials and often whole elements of the plan left out to save money. The Lakeshore Drive modernism of Mies van der Rohe in Chicago (which used the best of everything, including real estate and views) does not compare. At Pruitt-Igoe, low cost and low services were the primary design considerations (Birmingham: 295). Therefore, any association with "modernism" was ideological, because modernism, deployed neutrally, really meant "bourgeois modernism". A deeply structural anti-Utopia was at work.

The example is crucial for our genealogy of contemporaneity as it illustrates a variety of the modern nowhere to be found in today's scene. It was a failure (and one of Yamasaki's greatest professional regrets), to be sure, but only because it tried to succeed. For the example to make sense within the context of contemporaneity, we need to examine not just the design process but also the precise socio-historical moment of Pruitt-Igoe. It is the latter that has gone under-discussed in accounts of this phenomenon of architectural history. Elizabeth Birmingham's work goes some way to filling this gap. Birmingham's long essay on Pruitt-Igoe, and critique of Jencks, tries to shift the emphasis on design and modernistic "modes of reading", which Jencks interpreted onto another plane of thought (namely, racial segregation) as something to be realised and controlled through architecture. The complex had many problems that were not simple "design issues", but social planning ones: "The final plan designated the Igoe apartments for whites and the Pruitt apartments for blacks. Whites were unwilling to move in, however, so the entire Pruitt-Igoe project soon had only black residents" (Hoffman). Birmingham writes:

> [T]he ascendant myth that traces the failure of high modernism to the demolition of Pruitt-Igoe by asserting that the focus on poor people's inability to "read" high modernism, and hence Pruitt-Igoe, is not simply shifting the grounds of an argument that needs to be about race and poverty. It is also simply wrong. The residents of Pruitt-Igoe read and de-coded that housing project perfectly, recognizing it for what it was—an urban reservation which had the effect of containing and segregating those residents from the rest of the city and the city's resources. (1999: 291–309)

Birmingham brings the notion of "structural racism" into the debate to contradict the comfortable picture Jencks had drawn that concluded with the high cultural problem of how different groups "read" architecture. In other words, the project did not fail because its users were not trained in reading architecture. Jencks posits the principles of modernism as primarily cognitive rather than lived, bodily, socio-economic, and racialised. Furthermore, as Birmingham reveals, the "community never materialised" not because of failed design but rather because of the actions of the Housing Authority, which rewarded tenants for informing on the activities of other tenants. Without wanting to apologise for the architecture, each building must be cast in light of a complex of things to do with processes that are at once social, racial, and ultimately linked to the realities of capital, ownership, and distribution that lie at the secret centre of Utopian desire. Here we are dealing with an example of a modernist architecture at the service of an élite ("the rest of the city"), that still believed that contemporaneity was something to be overcome in itself; that is, with an accompanying vision of a different future to be consciously brought into being. The Pruitt-Igoe scheme is notable, however, as a late moment that saw modernism and the ethic of the future intersecting, because of its status as a state-centred attempt—however failed—to develop the world beyond the ideals of large businesses and private interests. (It is expected that major architectural projects in terms of housing displaced populations, on the rise in the new century, will want to be imagined outside of the modernist Utopianism of Yamasaki, but will also want to learn from it.)

## DOWN WITH THE "FRONTIER OF THE SKY"

The intention of the next two sections is not to provide an overview of the situation of architecture in the aftermath of the events of 11 September, 2001 and the subsequent Anglo-American invasion and occupation of cities in Afghanistan and Iraq, which, to a large extent, along with the "Arab Spring" and the ongoing European economic crises, characterise the geopolitical situation of the new century. Such an overview of the global architectural situation is virtually impossible (Terry Smith's *The Architecture of Aftermath* proposes some good generalisations, however). The intention here is to to renew the critical context for the way in which the event of the rebuilding of lower Manhattan is conceived in public discourse, by reflecting on Yamasaki and the practice of Lebbeus Woods. The Silverstein-Libeskind project—by completion, significantly compromised—in lower Manhattan exemplifies a colossal lack of imagination and compromise in its proposed return to tradition by deploying the form of a huge tower. Architecture has been reduced to image insofar as the end product is a Libeskind project by name only, and by image. The aura of the auteur architect (personal narrative, signature style, signature ethics) remains to legitimise a fundamentally alienated process.

The tower is designed to achieve the ultimate height of 1,776 feet, which is a number that has been chosen in homage to the founding of the United States of America. This is a cheap and naïve incarnation of a mix between Jewish Kabbalah and American symbolism. The figure is difficult to justify economically and seeks to express power, prestige, and American national history. This work wishes to be read in terms of national power, but is more appropriately read as a radical signification of nostalgia for what the US used to be, and ignores a situation that is radically incomplete and incommensurate. This is architecture of national self-doubt in the guise of national pride.

The critic and curator Okwui Enwezor was quick to connect architectural form and politics after the WTC twin towers were destroyed: "the skyscraper is today obsolete not because of its lack of functionality and efficiency, but rather, as a modern emblem of progress it has entered into a stage of uncertainty" (2003: 107). He writes, "today it may in fact appear not only conservative but also reactionary", signalling a final end—theoretically, socially, and practically—to the once marvelled "frontier of the sky" (2003: 107).

It is no accident that we consistently return to Koolhaas' writings on New York. The "frontier of the sky" was one of modernity's great architectural conquests in the form of the tower and the high-rise: structures that have constituted the Ur-form of the late capitalist skyline. In *Delirious New York,* Koolhaas reflected on the capitalist-Utopian value of these forms: "the Skyscraper as utopian device for the production of unlimited numbers of virgin sites on a single metropolitan location" (1994: 83). Floor upon floor of identical rooms could now be created on a small land plot—the mass production of vertical space. Previously, anything above level two of a building was considered unfit for commercial usage and floors above the fifth uninhabitable. It was a developer's dream come true to be able to multiply value so economically with the arrival of Elisha Otis' elevator in the 1870s, to turn empty air into real estate in the theoretically endless addition of floors that required no tedious legwork.

From the beginning, this internal transportation machine lent itself to a community in immense layered grids floating above the city. Combined with the arrival of air-conditioning, its residential future was the state mass-housing solution on the one hand, and designer luxury apartments on the other. From this combination of technologies, what emerges is the possibility of a "street in the sky", a hermetic community columned high above ground, and a new form of congested existence. The most marvellous were to have shopping streets suspended inside, such as Le Corbusier's Unite d'Habitation. For the cognitive life of the residents it was a specifically "modern" experience that combines, in a sort of paradox that Baudelaire would have liked, intimacy and anonymity in the same space. Residents are close but apart, within touch but out of reach, physically present but emotionally absent. The characteristics of the street and crowd transferred into the sky.

Critics frequently associate the end of Utopia in modern architecture with the end of modernity itself; notably, one such was the architecture historian Charles Jencks, and the numerous uncritical repetitions of his all too brief analyses, however rich in insight. It is timely to note that Yamasaki's WTC buildings were premised on the Utopianism of the West, the grand narrative of North America, and Manhattan in particular as the centralisation point of world trade and emerging globalisation. Its full-blown destruction was a sure symptom of the West's waning power, its openness to question. If today the tower as a form is heralded in terms of "progress" or "freedom", which was the official narrative around the rebuilding project, it is conceivable that the current regime has begun to exploit in architecture the collective, emotive impulses and reserves of pre-"war-on-terror" times that are still collectively at work, however unconscious, in the present. The rebuilding of Ground Zero in the image of a big tower does not to create anything new, but refers back to the safety of the immediate past (not Yamasaki, but something close) and American national origins (simplified nostalgia for singularity rather than hybridity). It is the mark of what Bloch called "non-contemporaneity" in *Heritage of Our Times*, and a refusal to confront the contradictions of the present, contradictions that question the definition of "architecture" understood as mere built object.

The "abstract and structurally daring" (Koolhaas 2004e: 237) towers of Yamasaki's WTC brought modernism to its apotheosis in New York upon completion in 1972. (Incidentally, the same year Pruitt-Igoe was demolished.) The edifices were twins so large they dominated the skyline but did not really "participate" in it (Koolhaas 2004e). They exemplified what the architect called "Bigness": a condition of the large in which architecture competes with the city rather than contributes to it (an overwhelming feature of shopping "centres"). Enwezor has argued that the events of September 11, 2001 took the comfortable West by surprise, with the strongest shift of the margin to the centre in our time. Of course, the centre responded by invading two countries, Afghanistan and Iraq, and declaring a ubiquitous, absurd war on an emotion (namely "terror") that has resulted in far greater bloodshed than the New York and Pentagon attacks.

Elizabeth Grosz is one theorist who demands us to "*think* architecture otherwise" when architecture has strangely become America's metaphor for returning to a solid ground that is likely gone forever. It is a challenge to architecture historians as much as architects. It is a question "[t]hat cannot and should not be answered but must be continually posed, rigorously raised in such a way as to defy answers, whenever architecture ... sinks comfortably into routine, into formulas, accepted terms, agreed upon foundations, an accepted history of antecedents, or a pre-given direction" (Grosz: 58). Trade remains the West's naturalised future (however complex and problematic the "West" may have become). The WTC was originally conceived as a kind of achieved Utopia of conspicuous trade, and gave strong, practical architectural form to the contents of emergent global capitalism. "World trade" would have to be radically rethought to connect, in Anthony Vidler's terms, to "the housing question that still haunts architecture and development on a global scale" (2004: 147). The WTC—unlike that other great invention of the Cold War years, the Internet, focused on dispersed information that could survive a nuclear attack on the US (see Sterling's "A Short History of the Internet")—was a big centralisation machine and thus prone to attack from its conception: arborescent, in Deleuzian terms, not rhizomatic. Yamasaki wrote:

> [T]he legislatures of the two states [New Jersey and New York] directed the Port Authority to construct a World Trade Centre, to bring together the activities of private firms and public agencies engaged in world trade in one central location, thus facilitating international business contacts among the members of the foreign-trade community of this country's major port. The centre's intent is to provide communication, information, proximity, and face-to-face convenience for exporters, importers, freight forwarders, customs brokers, international banks, and the many other enterprises involved in world trade. (112)

If the skyscraper as an emblem of progress has entered a terminal stage of uncertainty, it should have been alarming that the winning design of the Port Authority of New York's competition held quickly after the event of destruction included a rhetorically strong (and very big) Freedom Tower. The name alone embodies either an oxymoron, or the reification of "freedom" as architecture. As Koolhaas has suggested, the competition was not intended "to restore the city's vitality or shift its centre of gravity, but to create a monument at a scale that monuments have never existed (except under Stalin)" (2004e: 239). It is an attempt to symbolise control, or a substitute for control, in a situation of uncertainty.

Unavoidable in any discussion of these matters is the (now significantly altered, some would say compromised) plan adapted from Libeskind's original design: the Freedom Tower plus a circle of related buildings. His circle motif was supposed to contradict New York's famed modernist grid, a mere formal game that is a far cry from Grosz's call for "*thinking* architecture otherwise", which means going beyond planning a mere built object. His design won in a furore of praise for its rhetoric of memory and trauma and narrative of freedom, light, and memorialisation (Lahiji 2004). Indeed, there is also a visual rhetoric to the design that refuses the heaviness of structures coming down into the street and city. The artists' impression of the Freedom Tower, widely circulated in the media, is a colourful, shining, almost floating installation, looking more like a giant hologram than an actually built, everyday mega-tower of glass and steel standing apart from the city. The narrative of an aggressive phallus has also been gently silenced (or perhaps it is too obvious), so too its function to perpetuate the hegemony of US global trade, which retains an aura of inevitability (even after the erasures brought on by the GFC and its repercussions).

The Freedom Tower (renamed in 2009 as One World Trade Center or 1WTC, a name that is arguably more nostalgically fraught, timid, and neutering than Freedom Tower), with its monolithic spike stretched aloft, was designed to mirror the nearby Liberty's torch but rather recalls Kafka's imaginative perversion of her torch in the opening pages of his novel *America* that sees it replaced by a sword (13). Symbolically, one might say, the spike reflects less the torch of Enlightenment than it does the sword of empire, or of an empire that is falling into nostalgia and ruin—an empire under erasure—which reveals the project as a symptomatic one. It is the work of Lebbeus Woods that perhaps best exemplifies a response to Elizabeth Grosz's call for an architecture that is "otherwise" in Woods' own proposal for the Manhattan site.

## PIRANESI OF THE CONTEMPORARY

The Freedom Tower (or One World Trade Center) in downtown Manhattan is a work of monolithic architectural nostalgia—among the greatest works of longing for lost time ever, if perhaps only profound in terms of scale. The architectural development of Ground Zero, the site where Yamasaki's twin towers once stood, had no choice but to be publicly justified in progressive terms, however misleading. Developer Larry Silverstein's compromised adaptation of architect Daniel Libeskind's design for the site provides us with a structure that is not Utopian, nor dystopian, but nostalgic for the near-past; that temporality that is said to be least accessible to us. Nostalgia may be here understood as the inverse of Utopia: a groping for what was rather than what might be.

The American architect Lebbeus Woods (1940–2012) left behind a significant body of work that offers a critical architecture, proposing a fresh distance on the reality of construction going ahead throughout the period of the contemporary, refusing, as he did, the existing terms of modernism and postmodernism. His refusal to think in already existing terms allows for a questioning of the deployment of architecture and restoration today. His own unofficial proposal for the site provides a rethinking of the mega-tower as a form harking back to the avant-garde cognitive renewal of what architecture might be. In the spirit of Russian Constructivism, Fredriech Kiesler, Archigram, and the Italian Superstudio group, and above all, earlier by centuries, Piranesi, we find a demand in Woods' practice of what he once referred to as "anarchitecture": that architecture be thought otherwise, theoretically endless, perpetually unfinished, and always negotiating a novel relation to the present. In other words, to paraphrase Jameson, architecture may have entered a phase in which we cannot imagine it except as ending, and whose "future seems to be nothing but a monotonous repetition of what is already here" (2003: 76).

The intriguing and multifaceted, yet oddly under-discussed, career of Lebbeus Woods (which obviously has everything to do with the fact that he did have any of his works built in his lifetime, but worked solely within the experiments of models, artworks, monuments, and provocative writings) has been characterised by a refusal to accept the continuation of architecture as it is. The subversive aspect to his work was consistently so strong that his designs refused the conventions of engineering, offering images that stand alone in the scene of architecture as sites of impossibility. Woods was not a Utopian, however, and was, it seems, less interested in jostling multiple or totalised futures into view (a task perhaps better suited to science fiction film and the novel) than he was with indirectly indicating what he called in *Anarchitecture* "indigestibility": an aesthetic based on the resistance to being consumed by a system (Woods 1992: 142). His drawings, models, installations and writings gravitate towards the emergent and the new, but also the turbulent and difficult-to-consume past. They are temporal constructions. One is aware of a deep effort to maintain the *difficulty* of the past, its complexity as a field of frictions that do not permit nostalgia to take hold. Nostalgia may be critiqued as a fetish of the past where a partial view takes over and becomes the whole.

Throughout his work, Woods was preoccupied with his own vocabulary of architectural thinking, mostly involving the oft-unstated connections between architecture and war, which he based, after the tradition of the "social body" and the "body politic", on the human body in various states of damage and repair—the city as a kind of "war body". In his writings, he claimed the tabula rasa of modernism—the wiping of the slate for fresh construction—to be a serious loss to culture, arguing against the common sense notion of restoration. Woods grasps "restoration" as a terrible version of erasure because of the way in which simple reconstruction of what was already in place negates and conceals the fact that an event transpired; it has a silencing operation. For Woods, more complex states of time in architecture were possible. He wrote: "Wherever the restoration of war-devastated urban fabric has occurred in the form of replacing what has been damaged or destroyed, it ends in parody, worthy only of the admiration of tourists" (1993: 10). He proposed that ruins be deployed rather than swept up and cast aside, challenging the idea of always building on a clean surface, a modernistic absolute new beginning. (Jencks expressed a similar sentiment for Pruitt-Igoe: "Without doubt, the ruins should be kept, the remains should have a preservation order slapped on them, so that we keep alive a memory of this failure in planning and architecture" [9].) Woods (1993) noted that it would be comforting to find pleasant metaphors to describe the processes of "building on the existential remnants of war" but this would betray the work's character. He proposed an architecture of "scabs" and "scar construction", "abrasions" and healing as a deep process, not a "cosmetic" one. He wrote in *War and Architecture*:

> Ragged tears in walls, roofs, and floor structures created by explosions and fires are complex forms and figurations, unique in their history and meaning. No two are alike, yet they all share a common aspect: they have resulted from the unpredictable effects of forces released in the calculated risks of war. They are the beginnings of new ways of thinking, living, and shaping space. (1993: 10)

The site of Ground Zero was quickly recoded as an "empty" space in the long, difficult clean-up effort at the end of 2001. For Woods, the preliminary tabula rasa had already been realised, and the initial potential for embodied memory erased, meaning his proposal for the site departs from his rhetoric of "scar construction". It was too late for that (the temporary tourist apparatus that for a long while stood at Ground Zero notwithstanding). Yet, Woods proposed an alternative to the Freedom Tower—diagnostic or critical, rather than symptomatic.

In Woods' own "intentionally abstract … architecturally

incomplete" (2004b: 34) design for the WTC site, he posed a provocation to a culture that cannot think Utopically, and whose only foreseeable historical future is the "more and more" structure of consumer capitalism, with its regime of celebrity and competition. The architect critiqued the whole approach of architecture after 9/11. He wrote:

> When the World Trade Center towers fell, the only question obsessing architects was who would be commissioned to rebuild them. What could have been a great moment of debate about the relationship of architecture to the city, indeed, of the state of architecture as an idea and practice, was lost. In its place was a media spectacle to which many of the best architects docilely submitted, sacrificing substance to celebrity. But that is it: in the emerging monological culture, one deprived of dialectic and dialogue, dissention does not count. You are either with us or against us. You are either in the game, or you are out. (2004b: 19)

It is no accident that Woods' own design—so intellectually stimulating, even playful—was not part of the competition and had to be independently published as a book entitled *The Storm and the Fall*. It is a purely imaginative vision, or an "experimental architecture" to use Woods' preferred term (Myers, 5), not a "plan" or "finished form" but a concept (Woods 2004a: 34). In Jameson's terms, we could say it embodies the Utopian impulse, "that monumental part that cannot be the whole and yet attempts to express it" (2005: 4).

Woods' proposal for a new WTC exemplifies an anti-anti-Utopian position; it is a building that is in a state of incompletion and "remains perpetually under construction, and its ultimate height is not yet known" (Woods 2004b: 77). Again, connecting architecture to the realm of the living, not static, he deploys the rhetoric of "growing". The architect proposes less a discrete built object than an organisational structure. Woods names it the "World Centre": packed with rentable space, offices, public and private housing, as well as shopping malls, commercial facilities, sports and recreation, and so on, with several interlocking systems of internal mass transit that link to Manhattan horizontally underground. The main feature is a "vertical memorial park" called the Ascent that not only permits four experiences, but offers a complete rethinking of how architecture relates to the city. Woods states:

> The Pilgrimage (one month) is for the devout and consists of traversing a difficult vertical path through a series of stations, ordered by a narrative of the events and aftermath of 9/11. The Quest (one week) is for the ambitious and consists of a series of climbs up near-vertical faces, ledges, resting places, and camps ... The Trip (two or three days) is for the vacationer, with or without family, and consists of a series of platforms, lifts, escalators, interactive displays, hotels, restaurants, vistas, and educational entertainment ordered by the story of 9/11, and the histories of New York City, the skyscraper, and urban life. The Tour (half a day) is for day tourists and consists of a rapid elevator ride to the summit of the park. (2004a: 77–78)

Woods organises his vision/super-structure into a series of existentially distinct experiential layers. They range from the slow and difficult ("climbs up near-vertical faces") to swift intensities of experience ("elevator ride to the Summit"), thus allowing for levels of devotion in a theological sense. It is a subtle critique and does not propose a radically new system, but defiance of the singular temporality involved in the actually existing quick competition and reproduction of the site, which has been product-focused from the beginning. Most significantly, Woods remains an architectural thinker, not succumbing to the way out of the "expanded field" of today's contemporary art. This work, like his best projects, seeks an altering of conditions from within the discipline of architecture.

In a sense, the project is an elaborate spoof on the conceptual limitation of designs submitted into the competition—the images in his proposal are high concept—gestures, not plans—evocative rather than suggestive of the next practical step toward construction. The obvious exclusion of the word "trade" from the name of the building—the World Centre—inherits a strong sense of the globalisation of the late twentieth century ,but tries to remove the association of imperialism that Lenin connected to international trade in its highest form. However, as long as the so-called World Centre—as much as the United Nations headquarters—is located not simply in New York but in the United States at all, one has to seriously question its effectiveness as a contributor to a different kind of world, as architecture sunk in a quagmire of neo-liberalism.

This ambiguous proposal recommends the continuity of the (now reactionary, according to Enwezor) skyscraper to mega-dimensions. It recommends a critical state of perpetual becoming, reminiscent of Friedrich Kielser's "endless house" or Superstudio's "continuous monument"—the latter, a brutally epic concrete structure that wraps across the oceans joining distant cities, but in the same thought recommends impossibility. The failure of Woods' invention lies in its structural complicity with the skyscraper form itself, a continuation of the myth of Western society's phallic superiority. Indeed, the World Centre is intended to grow perpetually and always be the tallest building in the world. The World Centre, then, like the Anglo-American "war on terror", was conceived as having no end. The Centre is a monument therefore to the ideology of permanent contemporaneity, unlike, for instance, a monument to WWI that always has a delimited time period (1914-18). Woods' monument to "the contemporary" must be read over and against Libeskind's Freedom Tower, which is nostalgic for the "age of America" and modernism itself.

Earlier in modern history, we may recall that monuments were erected retrospectively, when events ended, rather than when they began, prospectively. Possessing a definite beginning (2001) but no end, the Freedom Tower (or One World Trade Center) resembles monuments to Stalinist leaders; think, for instance, of the North Korean example, "Kim Il-sung, 1912-Infinity". Woods, in line with the architects in the competition, has not conceptualised the "waning power of New York" (Koolhaas' phrase) as the centre of contemporary culture in its properly global dimension, but he has offered a complicated relationship between architecture and time, notably from within the discipline of architecture, not outside of it in the freer, more autonomous and potentially less commercial discipline of "art". The subversiveness of his project is enhanced by its lack of seriousness on a highly serious topic. As the new WTC is treated to mediatic spectacularisation, challenging the continuation of things as they are is imperative (which means finding ways to *think architecture otherwise*), Woods' work emerges to show us that a rethinking of how things are, no matter how implausible, is still a possibility.

Finally, it must be asked in discussions of the rebuilding of lower Manhattan, where is the reciprocal debate, and reciprocal design proposals, about architectural reconstruction in Kabul, Baghdad, Falluja, and the other brutalised Afghan and Iraqi cities that have seen a kind of daily 9/11 on their streets in the past decade? The best-resourced global building and architectural firms—the ones busily redoing the WTC, the ones that "prepared" Beijing for the 2008 Olympics and London in 2012, or those still creating the consumption-paradise called Dubai—have not been redeployed to rebuild the war-torn cities, to create fresh infrastructure, nor above all to propose architectural solutions to the "housing crisis which, unless addressed as a matter of urgency, could well assume catastrophic dimension" (UN-HABITAT: 1). The funding of repression that is American military occupation has not transferred to the funding of new growth. The ancient question— the decision to build housing or munitions, weaponry, or "livingry" (Buckminster Fuller's coinage)—remains a staple for any understanding of the asymmetrical architectural situation in "the contemporary".

## KOOLHAAS IN BEIJING

In November 2006, the Museum of Modern Art in New York (MoMA) department of design and architecture held an exhibition entitled *OMA in Beijing: China Central Television*

*Headquarters by Rem Koolhaas and Ole Scheeren.* The exhibition, like most of the MoMA's curatorial projects, continued in the line of the ideology of the autonomy of innovation, and the autonomy of the aesthetic. Descriptions of the kind the MoMA puts forth exist in the service of a fundamental aim: namely, to shift the aesthetic into the realm of the Absolute, which stands alone as incomparable. The function of the MoMA's exhibit was to enshrine the CCTV project with the merits of artistry above possible economic, political, and other extra-aesthetic qualities that the institution may be willing to mention in passing but ultimately rejects as subordinate to the advancement of art. For the MoMA, the CCTV project is significant for its status as "one of the most visionary undertakings in the history of modern architecture". To be sure, the reification of the aesthetic is a convenient way of not having to talk about the unsavoury and authoritarian nature of the client, who undoubtedly has intentions to rock the world far beyond that of the immediacy of the built object easily submitted to visual circulation within the iconomy. The image of the object itself, however, does have an important function that serves the institution and the state; the architecture provided by the OMA is a formal rendering of power, I argue, in both the actual constructed space of the city and within the economy of image. CCTV is not an exception among instances of spectacle architecture; it gives form to an otherwise diffuse and centreless power.

This section is not about the MoMA exhibition, but the *use* to which the institution—and other cultural sites—has put the image of the new CCTV headquarters: a deployment that is pre-empted by, or formatted into, the very construction of the building, and the relative freedom that star architects have to focus on the design of shape, icon, and landmark at the expense of the program and all forms of economic and political consequences that the development of a work of architecture such as CCTV can possibly have. The CCTV project is about the conspicuous display of power, pure and simple, and Koolhaas and the OMA are its collaborators.

The OMA and China are aware that media represents

power and that control of the image in contemporaneity may mean control of reality. The deceptively classical symmetry of the company's dualism, OMA/AMO, is focused, on the one hand, on architecture—that is, designing and producing buildings—and on the other, anti-architecture—that is, taking architecture beyond itself in the form of a think tank. In Bruce Sterling's words, AMO is "devoted to the virtual" (2003: 167). Sterling draws a distinction between OMA and AMO as that between, respectively, physical buildings and "information". Between these two realms of practice, Sterling argued, "there is less and less distinction to be made"; physical buildings are frequently designed on computer screens and information—unruly and sprawling in the contemporary world—"cries out for shelter and disciplined organisation". This may be the case, but Sterling's simplification is drastic. Above all, what the construction of CCTV might be called upon to illustrate is the incredible disjuncture between the output of AMO and OMA; the critical work of the AMO is not continued in the buildings. The ideas in each interact, but they are not illustrative of each other.

The OMA, since its initial success in the 1990s, has accepted increasingly bigger and more ambitious individual building projects. CCTV is perhaps the most visible; it is certainly the largest, itself a thesis in *bigness*. Located in Beijing's new CBD, the CCTV is a megastructure encompassing approximately 558,000 square metres of floor-space designed as the new headquarters for China's state television broadcaster. While CCTV is an icon of instantaneity, it carries with it a longevity that the Olympic buildings, conceived in the same era, do not. CCTV was not technically part of the 2008 Olympic redevelopment of the city, but it was timed to be complete for use at the Olympics of that year. As a building, its manifest innovation is to provide the entire process of TV-making—news and broadcasting, administration and offices, services, research, education, and program production—in a *continuous loop* of interconnected activities. Two towers rise from a common platform and:

[J]oin at the top to create a cantilevered penthouse for the management. A new icon is formed: not the predictable 2-dimensional tower "soaring" skyward, but a truly 3-dimensional experience, a canopy that symbolically embraces the entire population: an *instant icon* that proclaims a new phase in Chinese confidence. (AMO 2004: 489, emphasis mine)

A number of themes emerge with the new building that resonate with the modern and with that different but related phenomenon, modernisation: the Utopian expenditure of a great metamorphosis of form (the loop) and the suddenness of its arrival. Instantaneity is a key issue at work in the new development, this immense (and uniquely national) foregrounding of the modern spirit. Modernisation is, as Jameson has argued (2002: 166), more a repetition than an invention, that can only be performed today with immense resources of historical self-awareness.

The building itself was said to contribute to the "coherence" of the organisation and, in a physical chain of interdependence of departments, to offer "solidarity" instead of isolation between the parts of the organisation. (Previously, they were distributed randomly and *generically* across the city.) The *loop* is conceived as a public space—something the old headquarters did not have; visitors are admitted and can "freely" circulate within its secured interior, separated off from the private spaces of production. But, for this ideology, CCTV [Chinese Central Television] represents a limit, as Murray Fraser has argued:

[CCTV] contains a public right of way snaking through its contorted form [that] does not as such challenge the notorious secrecy and authoritarianism of that state-controlled institution. It offers at best an isolated symbol of critique, rather than a critical architecture that can hint at changes in meaning through radical aesthetics and a thoroughgoing spatial manipulation of the building programme. (Fraser: 333–34)

This is basically compiling the known and the obvious. CCTV presents a contradiction. It does not seem to advance the AMO's project to take architecture beyond itself; rather, it affirms the continued existence of the individual building. It goes against the discourse pouring out of both Koolhaas and the AMO. It is a massive built object, affirming the most classical, heroic, monumental aspect of the discipline. It is also a testament to the linked nature of the OMA and AMO. They fuel each other.

The OMA has tended to build structures that not simply shelter but seek to intervene and invent conditions of new possibility. In developing a reading of CCTV, I will suggest Koolhaas' debt not to the radically different Mies van der Rohe or the Japanese Metabolists (oft-cited precursors), but to Yamasaki. CCTV is a useful example for invoking a connection between late modernism (not postmodernism) and the OMA. CCTV was designed by the OMA with Ole Scheeren, a Koolhaas disciple and partner, heading the project. It is an aggressively abstract building, not unlike Yamasaki's twin WTC towers (1972-2001) in this respect. This comparison is legitimated by Koolhaas' own constant gestures to the status of Yamasaki's WTC. Koolhaas, obsessed with New York City (witness *Delirious New York*) and, more recently, the twin towers, praised the fact that they were "abstract and structurally daring". Koolhaas also noted that "twinning [was] their only genius" (2004e: 237). Comparably, the "genius" of the CCTV design lies in the monumental form of its continuous loop, daring in its simplicity, its shape outlining a massive void.

Koolhaas has wrapped CCTV in a mythos of meaning involving the late WTC. As Koolhaas narrates the project, CCTV's form responds to the need for a new architectural possibility in the post-9/11 world, wherein the skyscraper no longer has the same meaning. We have already considered Enwezor's argument about the "stage of uncertainty" that the form of the skyscraper has entered (Enwezor 2003: 107). If in 1972 the completion of Yamasaki's World Trade Centre signalled the perfection of the skyscraper, then the genre was left with no future but replication; it had nowhere to go. As I have already argued, the WTC was conceived as a big centralisation machine—arborescent, not rhizomatic.

The WTC can be read as an attempt to symbolise control, or as a substitute for control in a situation of uncertainty, as it gave concrete form to America's central role within late or multinational capitalism. CCTV was conceived at the moment of the new WTC competition, in 2002, "not in the back-ward looking USA, but in the parallel universe of China" (Koolhaas, 2004f: 515). Koolhaas justified the OMA's decision not to participate in the WTC competition and to bid for China instead as one that favoured the Utopian over the nostalgic, or the future (China) over the past (the US). The WTC was identified with memorialisation and the CCTV (with China (and the world's largest market) having recently joined the World Trade Organisation) was identified with the opportunity to articulate and symbolise that country as a new world superpower. The decision is reduced to signature Koolhaas minimalism in the slogan used in *Content* (2004): "Go East".

The CCTV building is a spectacle-event designed to engineer spectacle-events—that is, to monopolise the gaze of huge televisual markets—internal to China and external in the world market. The OMA did not arrive in China from out of Europe and North America and start building in a state of disorientation. An information project preceded design. With OMA/AMO in China, the map preceded the territory; the Harvard Project on the City began in China, in 1994, with pure investigative research, which appears to have paid off (if built execution is the secret Utopia of AMO). AMO, as an ideological project, grasps that information is the rule of the day—compiling disinterested data, or content, to be retroactivated as capital in potential, not-yet conceived of future situations, almost as a kind of curriculum vitae for the future.

The titles alone of the big Koolhaas volumes are a giveaway of the historical transformation at stake here. The OMA participates in, even actively promotes, the transition from Communism to Consumer Capitalism, especially in the country's First Special Economic Zones. (Shenzhen and Zhuhai became official labs for free-market experiment under Deng.) Koolhaas' answer to Chairman Mao's *Little Red Book*, his own Big Red Book *Great Leap Forward* (with ironic gold coins stamped on the cover) charts the building boom in China's Pearl River Delta. (It perhaps suggestive that Koolhaas' is a book, and red, yet unlike Mao's infamous volume, it is too heavy to wave or carry in one's pocket.) The companion volume, *Guide to Shopping*, charts the now centuries-long rise of arcades, commercial plazas, and shopping malls that have become late capitalism's default mode of social space and key players in the post-war mutation of cities. In less than ten years, the OMA won the CCTV project for Beijing—the Office's biggest commission.

The building was timed to circulate as an image of power at the very moment that China occupied the world stage as host of the Olympics. It is a building designed to project, both inward to China and outward to the international community, as a sign of technological daring and state power; the Chinese media are among the least free and most censored in the world. Knut Birkholz reminds us that the history of architecture is, to a great extent, the structural demonstration of power, and CCTV is no exception.

> The reverse side to *bigness* and the "absence of characteristics"—irrelevance—appears to be something that Koolhaas does not fear. But the hybrid form that he so values metamorphoses everything it includes all too easily into a monotonous unity; the accumulated architectural effects compete for attention, like the metropolises, shopping malls, television programs and those architectural publications that must court an audience with their nice pictures. Should an especially beautiful building arise in Beijing, which is the express intention of Koolhaas, then this would be pure and simple prettification of the brutality of its surroundings. These surroundings make the entire project ugly in the true sense of the word, and whoever has good reason to hate the power of the state of China might follow a primordial reflex by directing their loathing against the

new icon. (Birkholz 2006)

The OMA, then, may have provided the Chinese masses with a kind of Bastille to storm. Icons in the current age have become useful—for insurgents, terrorists, the mass media, and tourists alike—for their target potential: a point brought home by Smith in *The Architecture of Aftermath*, in which he argues that the WTC towers were "more than symbols" and not a spectacular confirmation of postmodern analyses in which appearance triumphed over reality but "the actual buildings were central, tangible embodiments of the complex functions that they housed, the most visible point of concentration of the complex array of powers associated with them" (2006b: 7). Buildings of this kind, world trade centres or mass media production machines designed for global circulation as image, become images of power, but are also already, centralising machines that maintain power. Power, diffuse and mobile like information or digital light, needs architecture to present itself in the real, to give it form and place. Architecture in the contemporary continues to provide shelter, as architecture has always done, but of another kind—not that of human protection from the elements, but that of the vastly different "wilderness" of our time, the heterogeneous information disorder. Birkholz outlines the politically repressive context in which the OMA has agreed to build, citing the *Human Rights Watch* on China:

> Infringements against human rights in the form of violence against political dissidents, against representatives of various religious organisations, against those who provide support to the HIV infected or those suffering from AIDS, against Muslim minorities labelled as separatists in Xinjiang, against those who protest the illegal occupation of Tibet ... Freedom of assembly exists nowhere, strikes are smashed, justice is absent from the courts. Censorship rules supreme in all the mass media and, to a massive extent, on the Internet too. (Birkholz 2006)

I wish to conclude this section on a note that suggests that an oppositional architecture is possible, despite the limitations of CCTV. One way of going about this will be an insistence on the use of architecture in posing issues. Architecture, then, might be rethought as an open resource useful to those not directly in the art or business of development—a resource to inform the critical imagination. The AMO's briefs have tended to be focused around rethinking the definition of "architecture", which involves going beyond the discipline of architecture as the *practice of constructing buildings*. Architecture is a critical modality *per se*, a discipline capable of migration to the world outside of the discipline. One of the interesting implications of the current state of affairs is that at the exact moment of architecture's incredible triumph—more construction is currently underway globally that at any point in history—physical buildings themselves (the CCTV headquarters being no exception) have become the questionable centre of the field.

As the OMA sees it, one of the constant problems for architectural research when undertaken by architects is that it is reified by the particular project or client's interests and is stopped short of launching its own unique course. This is undoubtedly very frustrating for architects. The knowledge produced by an architect for a client, the argument goes, is the "opposite of an agenda", based on the architect's random sequence of commissions that it attains largely ad hoc from the system and its current needs and aims, whatever they might be. The function of a company such as AMO is crucial in this regard and has much to recommend it, although the model has not been widely adopted by architecture firms. Such a model is essential in taking the theorist from the materiality of the building to the conceptual, to the imagined, to the intangible, and to the reloading of agendas.

For a long time, the most interesting architects have tended to be those engaged not simply with designing and building but *writing*. Writing is a way of overcoming the problem of waiting for commissions. In periods of waiting, critically minded architects have regeared their attention toward propaganda. In the high modernist era, architects like Le Corbusier, Frank Lloyd Wright and, to some extent, Walter Gropius, offered parallel universes of architectural imagination to their built projects in treatises and manifestoes written variously to enlighten or obscure, sensitize or desensitize, reveal or push the limits and contents of what the discipline of architecture can be.

In this way, a generation before Koolhaas, in America, Robert Venturi changed the direction of architectural thought, not through buildings but through manifestoes: *Complexity and Contradiction in Architecture* and, especially, *Learning from Las Vegas*. At the most challenging, architectural discourse of this kind admirably seeks to redefine the imaginative and conceptual limits of what is too often a mundane practice of providing spaces for the powers that be and repeating that which already exists. The manifesto makes connections: unravelling visions of architecture into other disciplines or forms of culture, emphasising revolutionary potentials.

Recently in the history of architecture, Koolhaas and the OMA introduced a new kind of product/project: the big book publication, which is a way of launching research beyond the reifications from above imposed by clients. For Koolhaas, the "liberation" of publishing, as opposed to functional, slow and expensive construction, equals the possibility of rethinking or repurposing architecture as a form of relationship to the contemporary city. In 1995, Koolhaas's *S,M,L,XL*, totalling some 1,376 pages, was the inaugural text of this "genre", and the results of the Harvard Project on the City in China continued strong in its footsteps. These were manifestations of what might be called "Bigness by other means" and, in Hal Foster's terms, are "not coffee-table books, they are coffee tables" (2003: 22). They were not supplements to building, or even straightforward interpretations, but active, autonomous projects. The new books might be seen as architectural visions in their own right. We can reconceive architecture not as common sense individual buildings, or as mere style, but as *organisational structures* in their attempts to give form to an aspect of today's wilderness of information in all its "unthinkable complexity" (in William Gibson's sense).

Koolhaas and the OMA have achieved some of the most high profile built products of the last two decades. A short list of the OMA's "random sequence of commissions" (2004a: 20) would include: the redevelopment of Eurolille, the Seattle Public Library, the Guggenheim in Las Vegas and Guggenheim-Hermitage, Prada in New York, Casa da Musica in Porto, CCTV in Beijing, and a from-scratch "city" or city-simulation in Dubai (on hold due to the money crash). Koolhaas has worked in each case on the construction of narrative and concept around each of the buildings, generating occasionally compelling "scripts" for architecture. Whatever the status of Koolhaas as an architect, in the final analysis, he and his office are ambiguous entities. He is a committed theorist throughout his journey, which has helped highlight the contemporary intersection at architecture and the contemporary city. The originality of OMA derives from the fact that Koolhaas operates within the disciplinary binds of "architecture", but he is not strictly an architect. He has posed as a postcritical architect—that is, one who makes a critique only by participating in the system that one wishes to oppose. He does not see a dialectical outside, but only the inextricability of criticism and participation. The end to which this takes us, however, is far from heroic, in the sense that designing high tech infrastructure and architecture for totalitarian capitalism offers an alarming picture of the direction not simply of architecture but of the world. Architects are in a position to refuse; in fact, a politics of refusal and refusing to build may occasionally be the more radical option in the present political climate.

## DELIRIOUS DUBAI

Any discussion of contemporaneity in architecture eventually makes its way around to the phenomenon of construction in the Persian Gulf city-state of Dubai, where in the middle of the last decade approximately a quarter of the world's construction cranes were said to reside. The example of Dubai discredits the postmodern notion that the current age is one that is motored by *reproduction* rather than simple production, an idea increasingly difficult to sustain in view of the completely constructed environments either built recently, under development, or about to be developed in the UAE (those not cancelled by the money crash). This section responds to the generalised mythos of Dubai that is emerging which is, I contest, comparable to the historical mythos of New York (at the same time that it sends New York as an image and an example into the virtually cultural-archaeological past). I do not wish to discredit Dubai's example by referring to New York as a rough but useful precedent, but instead to mark out and insist upon Dubai's historic originality (which is more honest as well as more interesting). By far, a mythos does not indicate the existence of a false world, but the attempt to make a real one meaningful. For New York, I will limit my study mostly to Koolhaas' own myth-making manifesto, *Delirious New York.*

Koolhaas has been positioned—either by himself or by his investors—as the poster apologist for Dubai, willingly becoming not a writer of retroactive manifestoes for what has already happened, but a profoundly prospective provocateur: "It is particularly cruel that the harshest criticism [of Dubai] comes from old cultures that still control the apparatus of judgment, while the epicentres of production have shifted to other end(s) of the globe" (2007a: 7). In particular, Koolhaas is one of the lead figures behind the publication *Al Manakh*, a publishing project that sees AMO in collaboration with *Archis* and the Arab business research initiative Moutamarat. Probably because Koolhaas is an apologist for neo-liberal capital and because he wants to continue building bigger and bigger works of architecture—his planned construction for Dubai is a whole city island, a kind of homage to his beloved New York City—he must locate a rhetoric of escape from the critiques of others. Koolhaas writes:

[M]uch like Singapore in the 1980s and China in the

1990s, the recent development of the Gulf, particularly Dubai, has been met with derision: Mike Davis' damning "Walt Disney meets Albert Speer" echoes William Gibson's characterisation fifteen years ago of Singapore as "Disneyland with the death penalty" ... The recycling of the Disney *fatwa* says more about the stagnation of the Western critical imagination than it does about Gulf Cities (2007a: 7)

The sheer amount of from-scratch projects having recently been completed or that are underway in Dubai (or that the financial crisis has put on hold) and much of the Emirates would seem to contradict that particular (and prevalent) taboo of postmodern thought that views class as an entity that no longer exists, or no longer matters, in the same way as it did within the classical modernity that Marx experienced and wrote about. As a centre and spectacle of construction, wealth and consumption (with a focus on rescaled extremities of luxury, conspicuous excess, and fantasy environments) intended to out-scale all previous efforts in other parts of the world, Dubai surely does damage to the idea. As Georges Bataille might have argued, Dubai is about excess: conspicuous waste for its own sake and its own pleasure. In the moment of global historical climate crisis, it is disastrous, but also oddly fitting that the most advanced societies should pull together the resources to produce a pseudo-Utopia of pseudo-Utopias that signals the end of program in architecture—an entry into a moment in which the programmatic content of modernism and postmodernism (oddly alike in this respect) has not been negated, but simply left behind. Dubai signals the acceptance of a contradiction that is no longer perceived to be something to be solved.

Before forging my historical comparison with New York City, some preliminary sketch of Dubai is necessary that not simply indicates the unprecedented explosion of development in the region but that at once indexes some of the forceful imaginary constructs or concepts that helped to drive the incredible boom of the last decade. Koolhaasian Bigness is the unofficial "style" of Dubai; its growth its only "project". Of course, bigness is not really a style at all, but a condition that architecture enters into "beyond a certain scale" and can, in reality, take any form that is conceivable and constructible. It is a cliché that in Dubai, "if you can think of it, you can build it". There is a good reason for this, and it is part of the fact that, as Koolhaas himself puts it:

> We live in an age of completions, not new beginnings. The world is running out of places where it can start over ... Sand and sea along the Gulf, like an untainted canvas, provide the ultimate tabula rasa on which new identities can be inscribed: palms, world maps, cultural capitals, financial centres, sport cities ... . The Gulf's entrepreneurs are reaching places that modernity has not reached before (2007a: 7).

Dubai has grown out of a desert that, thirty years ago (so the circulating myth has it), saw only tents, a creek, and camels. The architecture historian Jennifer Taylor argues that Dubai, aspiring towards the status of "next generation destination" and the call that "the world has a new centre", is literally "building itself into significance", out of nothing (Taylor 2007). Koolhaas believed this as well: "The Gulf is not just reconfiguring itself; it's reconfiguring the world" (2007a: 7).

Mike Davis in the *New Left Review* essay "Fear and Money in Dubai" provides a useful overview of the sort of projects underway in this "strange paradise" (Davis 2006). For Davis, Dubai is a mixture of fantasy and gigantism (or bigness). Dubai is the centre of dozens of intentionally outlandish mega-projects including the artificial "island world" (a map of the mercator projection in the form of real-estate), the world's tallest building (intentionally superseding Taipei 101, which was, until recently, the world's tallest building), an underwater hotel, a major dinosaur park, the world's largest indoor ski slope (the world's largest refrigerator), and a hyper-mall that encompasses the world's largest continuous interior space. The biggest project—a mega-project of mega-projects—is Dubailand, which represents a delirious level of commercial entertainment speculation beyond that of the already extra-large Disney projects. Davis writes:

> Literally a "theme-park of theme-parks" it will be more than twice the size of Disney World and employ 300,000 workers who, in turn will entertain 15 million visitors per year ... Like a surrealist encyclopaedia, its 45 major "world class" projects include replicas of the Hanging Gardens of Babylon, the Taj Mahal and the Pyramids, as well as a snow mountain with ski lifts and polar bears, a centre for "extreme sports", a Nubian village, "Eco-Tourism World", a vast Andalusian spa and wellness complex, golf courses, autodromes, race tracks, "Giants' World", "Fantasia", the largest zoo in the Middle East, several new 5-star hotels, a modern art gallery and the Mall of Arabia. (2006: 48)

For a more astounding list of "imagineered urbanism" (a Disney model), works in progress, and projected works, one need only consult the "development atlas" in the "Gulf Survey" compiled by the AMO, forming a third of the *Al Manakh* collaboration (which also gives data on construction in Kuwait, Bahrain, Qatar, and Abu Dhabi). There is no point in trying to account for all of these here, and nor should the atlas be thought of as complete; such attempts to capture the scene are outdated before they are printed. (Before the GFC, the commentators' consensus was that one new mega-project was announced each week.) Of course, for the Marxist Davis, the fantasy has a dark underside of reality in the form of the plight of South Asian construction workers—something that falls outside of Koolhaas' vision. Indeed, whole suburbs that look like nightmare "radiant cities" have arisen to house the workers who are reportedly, in the worst instances, stripped of their rights.

Dubai City might be reframed in relation to New York City. Like historical New York, Dubai is a small place that has become host to some of the most rapid and ambitious architectural projects on the planet. The rise of New York City was the cultural, architectural and financial harbinger of twentieth-century modernity. The architecture of the twentieth-century is unthinkable without its example. According to Koolhaas, its development unfolded with unbelievable speed and in such a state of excitement that it had no time to reflect on itself as a "project". Unusually for a modernist development, New York had no manifesto, and it was up to the architect to write one retroactively. Koolhaas coined the term "Manhattanism" to embody the phenomenon of building and the "culture of congestion" that was unleashed on the tiny island from the late nineteenth-century up to the 1930s. Mike Davis usefully provides a comparative launch pad, as he writes, "Despite its blast-furnace climate ... and edge-of-the-war-zone location, Dubai confidently predicts that its enchanted forest of 600 skyscrapers and malls will attract 15 million overseas visitors a year by the year 2010, three times as many as New York City" (2006: 48). Is Dubai the reciprocal growth of the "waning power of New York"?[7]

The short ten-year time-span that can be called "the rise of Dubai" parallels the rise of New York within modernity in instructive ways. Of course, the comparison between these two remarkably different places, with outstandingly different histories and geographies, will have plenty of limitations. But the fact that Dubai is widely perceived as a phenomenon in development without precedent might be reason enough to begin to forge some initial set of markers that help to make the experiment meaningful. If New York can be conceived as an historical precedent to Dubai, it appears small-scale and relatively slow by Dubai's standards, but the shock of the new, and the awe inspired by simple pathbreaking endeavours for those contemporary witnesses, remains similar.

The enigma of Dubai—one that scarcely could have been imagined within industrial modernity—is that we do not have the global resources to construct and maintain the kind of place that is there in production. Dubai is about excessive

---

[7] The phrase belongs to Koolhaas from his post 9/11 post-script to the 1978 manifesto.

consumption, conspicuous design of the extraneous, the unneeded for its own sake, in the face of its opposite—incredible poverty and the global housing and food crises named by the United Nations. Koolhaas is adept at repeating the underlying intentions of this major investment in building. He writes: "The Gulf—its initial development triggered by the discovery of oil—is undergoing hyper-development to be ready for oil's eventual depletion" and "Gulf cities are in construction *now*. This means they are, inevitably, based on the repertoire of current urban prototypes—communities (themed and gated), hotels (themed), skyscrapers (tallest), shopping centres (largest), airports (doubled)—cemented together by Public Space, extended soon with boutique hotel, museum franchise and masterpiece" (2007b: 194). Against the critical perspective of Davis, Koolhaas privileges the *new* for its own sake:

> If you want to be apocalyptic, you could construe Dubai as evidence of the end-of-architecture-and-the-city-as-we-know-them; more optimistically you could detect in the emerging substance of The Gulf—constructed and proposed—the beginnings of a new architecture and of a new city. (2007b: 194)

The construction of attraction architecture and experience architecture in the form of hotels and entertainment complexes (including shopping) might be said to lack one thing that the "West" continues to monopolise: culture in the old sense, which is to say "culture" in the classical sense of the term—high or bourgeois culture. If Dubai is becoming the shopping capital of the Gulf, Abu Dhabi's strategy revolves around an investment in culture. Thomas Krens, who was until recently the director of the Guggenheim Museum company, is collaborating with Abu Dhabi on a vision for place as a cultural destination, with a planned, predictably Frank Gehry-designed Guggenheim Museum (a Guggenheim large enough to swallow other Guggenheims). The "vision" is supposed to offer the "next big step" after the Bilbao moment. In discussions about the development project, another part of the "futurised present" that is the most advanced part of the UAE and the Middle East itself can be seen.

The GFC and excess were not compatible, however. The money crash radically changed Dubai's trajectory. In the long term, however, it is not likely to have altered Dubai's ambitious project to keep building itself into significance to become a major, uniquely twenty-first century destination and dominant trading centre between the West and the Middle East. How long it will take Dubai—years or decades—to pull itself back into the previous position of excessive production is unknown. The narrative of Dubai has thus far been one of conceptualising, planning, announcing, and often building (or beginning to build) shock-inducing mega-projects based on conspicuous, capitalistic consumption. After the crash, Dubai has not stopped building, although many projects have been put on indefinite hold, such as Dubailand and several of the artificial island projects. The focus has shifted to something that Dubai risked ignoring: infrastructure, the sort of projects required to generate and sustain places but which are not particularly glamorous, shock-inducing, or even interesting as world news. As *The New York Times* reported: "Dubai keeps building, but soberly" (2010). Dubai has quietly begun construction on a new airport designed to rival Heathrow in scale, and a series of new highways. Dubai, it seems, is—partly due to financial bailouts rumoured to equal around 20 billion dollars from Abu Dhabi—readying itself for the next phase of global capitalism's expansion: the boom after the recession-ridden current era.

UNITED NATIONS IN THE SYSTEM BEYOND THE SYSTEM

In this final section, a political question is reframed as an architectural one: can we rethink global capitalism in the act of rethinking architecture? In his September 2006 address to the United Nations, the late Venezuelan President Hugo Chavez plugged Noam Chomsky's book *Hegemony or Survival*, referred to then-US President George Bush Jr. as "the devil", and made a call to relocate the UN Headquarters from New

York to Venezuela (Caracas, we may assume). Readers responded to the plug, with sales of Chomsky's book soaring. Media and debate in both pro- and anti-Chavez sources focused largely on the name-calling aspect of the speech, which was arguably its least interesting aspect (and that is saying something). For Chomsky, the major concern over the UN is that it has become, in words he takes from Francis Fukuyama, "an instrument of American unilateralism" (Chomsky: 29). However, Chavez's call to relocate means more than contesting this claim. I want to present what the call may mean for architecture, using Lebbeus Woods' definition of the discipline as the "instrument for the invention of knowledge through action; the invention of invention" (Woods 1992: 142).

Chavez said: "Let's be honest. The U.N. system, born after the Second World War, collapsed. It's worthless ... maybe we have to change location. Maybe we have to put the United Nations somewhere else; maybe a city of the south. We've proposed Venezuela" (Chavez: 232). This is a challenge to architects. No avant-gardist can ignore the following thought experiment: what form would the new UN Headquarters have to take in order to articulate the global contents of the system beyond that desired by Chavez and his contemporaries? Will architects, their firms, and schools respond to the profound, if dormant, architectural-political future within Chavez's call? Here is an invitation to play with its apparent edginess as a politico-historical concept and, above all, to potentially trump the old Corbusian design of the UN Headquarters in New York, which may now become a museum: a relic of the immediate post-Second World War, late modern, and the ways it imagined international relations, language, spatial and military-technological limitations.

Chavez unwittingly lent a degree of urgency to a question to which architecture in the twenty-first century is eventually going to have to face. Naturally, he did not make explicit comments on the subject of building or design, but within his speech we may find a subterranean call that has everything to do with architecture—above all, its responsibility to produce and enable differences in human reality, however divided and complex the realm of the "human" may have become (as registered in Woods' designs). Regarding the UN's physicality, Nancy Soderbergh, former US Ambassador to the UN, once said: "In many ways [the UN is] a direct throwback to the '50s. The building itself is a throwback to the '50s with [period] chairs and everything, and there are still a lot of people that are stuck with the ... mentality of North vs South, blaming the US for all their evils" (Fasulo: 125). Her comment on décor is not particularly deep, yet implies a connection between architecture and the reproduction of geopolitical mentality. It is often frankly observed that the building has peeling paint, faded furnishings, worn fittings, and so on, so it is therefore no surprise to learn that the "village" has undergone no reconstruction or renovation since opening. But it comes as a shock to learn that the institution cannot afford renovation and is not even well funded enough today to keep up maintenance. This should not weaken, but strengthen the call for revision, redesign, and, in particular, relocation.

It has always been a possibility that another nation could offer a more economical deal for the UN. Linda Fasulo put it in consumerist terms in her book-length study of the institution: "Just as sports franchises move from city to city in search of the best domed stadium, the UN could shop around for the best offer" (133). "Shopping around" is less than what Chavez desired, of course, but it does serve as a reminder that the institution does not naturally exist in New York. New York is an extremely expensive location. Chavez's proposal to relocate to revolutionary Venezuela should be taken very seriously, as it may resolve a multitude of problems (so that the real problems may then start). Is it too much to suggest that the UN's relocation is not a radical but merely moderate call for change? It is not a guarantee for fulfilling all the institution's postwar Utopian goals of world peace, but it may be worth a try. It would have to begin with a reimagining of what world space might be, and what cultural trajectories and withdrawals are possible in the representational apparatus of architecture in contemporaneity.

Architects must do their research and put their laboratories and assistants to work. But the idea of a "system beyond the system" is of course something quite other than the old peaceful planet that was the UN's classical teleological mission. The latent ideological implication in Chavez's speech was that the UN, now in America, is imaginatively sinking into a liberal-democratic quagmire, a kind of invisible acceptance of America as "home of nations". Its famed message to tourists that "you are now on international soil" is its biggest myth.

So it is that America and the world, or at least the so-called "international community", may have to finally abandon the nostalgia that New York is its permanent centre. The city was the centre in the middle of the twentieth-century, but things have changed since then. Only an outdated architectural determinist would argue that global social transformation will automatically follow the occasion of the new architecture, but of course that is not the goal. Instead, the idea is to rethink present international spatial relations in terms of a habitable space, a dwelling for struggle that lives up to a form of inventiveness of which the current UN is incapable. Architecture is the site of revisioning and reimagining. To begin theorising, we could do worse than to start in a Wittgensteinian way. To renovate the philosopher's cry, that "to imagine a language means to imagine a form of life". For architecture this means: "to imagine a building is to imagine a world".

This "cognitive map" of architecture within the conditions of contemporaneity has hopefully brought three aspects home for us. First, the map, or constellation, that accrues from the exemplary architectures here presented is intended to be temporal as well as spatial; the dualism of the modern and the postmodern have been deployed to illustrate the negative aspects of the contemporary condition—in particular, the lack of programmatic content that is part of the ontological makeup of "the contemporary" as it has been deployed within the past decade. Second, the map is obviously far from complete, but the intention of cognitive maps is not to aim for completion (which, in any case, is impossible within the system of multinational or enigmatic capital). Third, the event of architecture designed for existence within the iconomy adds a development that Jameson was not able to see in the 1970s when he was working on the concept (and reading Louis Althusser and Lynch). The spectacular work of architecture, which corresponds to each of my examples, is already involved in the construction of something like a cognitive map on its own terms, an exercise in the construction of identity out of nothing within the global system. (Again, witness the Bilbao example.) Cities under the weight of multinational capital have proceeded to develop along lines of the unique individual building, that part that cannot be the whole but which tries to express it (paraphrasing Jameson); it is an architecture, we may now say, of the Utopian impulse. This is far from the Utopian planning of classical modernism. Architecture, in the deployment of the iconic building, has become part of the race for recognition, for power, as a fight against obsolescence in a world heavily dependent on the symbolic and on image, which has become indistinguishable from production itself.

In respect to the enormity such a task implies, this is really only a prologue. These examples are treated in a summary way in order to give a picture of the uneven globalised architectural situation: a situation in which the same pool of star architects is called upon to negotiate their art in states that are simultaneously participants in global commodity culture, but are also politically non-synchronous. The figure of the architect has emerged as one that exercises maximal aesthetic autonomy at the expense of having no authority whatsoever over the contents of the structures they are called upon and willingly provide. We have not seen a picture of a critical architecture. It will be necessary to go beyond this provisional picture and map the broad urban preconditions and effects of these spectacularly aggressive and pseudo-heroic exemplifications of contemporary hegemonic architecture. The spectacle is the tip of the iceberg of the generic city and globalised urban reality (which has been so well articulated for contemporaneity by Mike Davis in *Planet of Slums*), which is abandoned to chaos under the transcendent force of the mega-building and the commodity fetish, iconicity, and the spectacular.

The example of Pruitt-Igoe is a limited one, but retains its significance within the narrative of twentieth-century modernity and also as an important part of Yamasaki's identity within the contemporaneity discussion. The mass-housing development stands as an example of Yamasaki and many interwar and immediate post-war architects (Welfare State architecture, for instance) operating as a modernist, still focused on an ethical content for major architectural works: the thought and critical belief that architects could take the resources of the capitalist system and redirect its fortunes to social goals. The attempt was futile in the end, and resulted, if anything, in a more severe, more efficient impoverishment of the working class and racial segregation than had quite been possible before. As Murray Fraser has noted, it was Manfredo Tafuri, the historian and critic, who "asked how it could ever be possible to use architectural design in any positive sense to transform the lives of ordinary people, so long as the exploitative nature of the capitalist system … still prevailed" (Fraser: 332). Yamasaki, in trying—Utopically, in the classical modernist sense— to critique capitalism from within ended up becoming one of its worst collaborators. A different kind of density and a different kind of icon was created in Yamasaki's World Trade Centre—by this stage, he was a pure collaborator to the system, giving his client exactly what was required: a monument to global finance capitalism, structurally daring and abstract like the American-based system itself.

Koolhaas' articulation of the CCTV project in China would be very different if it were not for September 11, 2001. Koolhaas used the aftermath as a resource for a development that may be long overdue: the reinvention of the skyscraper. That is the architect's rhetoric. The CCTV project, however, is reminiscent of Yamasaki's attempt to articulate the contents of financial capital in the 1970s, and to express and create an icon for Chinese power, daring, and engineering ingenuity. Both are performances of monumental heroism. Both are attempts to reintroduce a community that was previously fragmented (financially and televisually, respectively), and have a Utopian impulse just beneath the surface. They are attempts at concentration—to allow for the multiple functions in the one space and in the one architectural entity. They are big projects that intentionally are constructed for immediate entry into the iconomy, projects of image capital, signs of prestige and real power.

Dubai, by contrast, is not about power but conspicuous consumption—the consumption of excess—in the face of a planet that desperately needs to be rethought around a concept of a great collective project and a *relationship* to the future, instead of its wholesale forfeiting in the construction of unsustainable monuments to an already exhausted system. Dubai offers a picture of a whole new pseudo-Utopian world of the senses—witness the seven-star hotel concept—and of glorious materialisation and hallucinatory experiences. I think this example ought not to be treated in isolation from the uneven global system of which it is admittedly a part—a perspective that allows now for us to re-conceive of the whole construction effort (the whole investment in "Dubai" as a place and a brand) as a radical compensation for the impoverishment of the global capitalist system as it comes out of the twentieth-century, a new reality of hyper-urban squalor and mega-slums, a bright light of false hope within a bleak and broken world, a "planet of slums" in Davis' sense. Such a situation demands the creation of architectural solutions, not just the creation of empty commodified desires.

The juxtaposition of Pruitt-Igoe and the mega-projects underway in Dubai has hopefully been instructive. In the 1950s, the major spectacle of architecture involved a commitment to the future and an ethic of resolution of social and cultural crisis. In contemporaneity's most visible, most ambitious developments (each geared toward circulation within the iconomy, each ultra-aware of their potential status as destination brands) there is a modernism—an aggressiveness, a pseudo-Utopian drive to reconfigure local and global space—but none of the ethical dimension of a Pruitt-Igoe. The disjuncture is related, of course, to the general absence of state developments and the enormity of capital in the hands of a few private big-visioned developers at this time. Dubai, with its absurd ski resorts in the desert is a symbol of the incredible level of excess that has been reached within the contemporary system. Dubai imagines itself not as a place that might resolve global contradictions, but as a place beyond those contradictions, as if it were in an autonomous zone of production and consumption immune from the increasingly obvious limits to global resources, of which it has been absorbing amongst the most of any state on the planet.

## 05: Endgame
### Consequences of Contemporaneity

> The sands of non-contemporaneous time are running out. Everybody lives, or is soon going to live, under conditions of global contemporaneity and has an undeniable right to be in the present time.
>
> Wolf Schafer

The writing of genealogies of contemporaneity is an attempt to see the global era of "the contemporary" as part of longer temporalities; indeed, as argued via Jameson, "the contemporary" is not a concept, but a narrative category. To insist that the contemporary is incomplete might open up the future once more as something that is different from the present, which also then means adopting the more radical position that we are not contemporary now—that we have never been contemporary. The preceding analyses of the contemporary and contemporaneity can be understood in a Deleuzian fashion—that is, as problems to think with rather than as absolute propositions. We have moved all the way from the "modern promises" of a collective project using the technological developments of modernity and the most progressive social projects (roughly from the eighteenth and nineteenth centuries onwards) to the distortion of such ideals in the form of the actually-existing-Utopia of "Delirious Dubai". It is, of course, an ironic Utopia. How will the contemporary of today be read by the alternative civilisation of the future? It seems necessary to be dissatisfied with the contemporary and to acknowledge that just because we exist now, or at the same apparent time, does not mean we are contemporaries. The United States is anything but contemporary, but it insists on trying to remake others in its own image.

We have seen that the contemporary (as an attitude of modernity) has a legitimate history in the resources of thinkers, in all of their ideological differences, from Kant's answer to the question "What is enlightenment?" to Baudelaire, Nietzsche, and on to Wyndham Lewis, to Bloch, through to Foucault and then Jameson, Marc Augé, Wolf Schafer, and Terry Smith. This is an odd path through a long history (and, yes, full of omissions). By arcing back into the past, as far back as the European enlightenment and the era of European power, we are able to assemble versions of a contemporaneity with content, or, specifically, of a modernity. Modernity was understood then as a way of relating to the present moment, as a form of commitment to the present in order to bring about another possible world, or Utopia. Such a "project" has not been without its excesses and atrocities, as we have seen, especially in the twentieth-century. When modernity gets botched, it botches everything.

In postmodernity, we saw less a "period" than a *moment* in the ongoing, radically uneven, and unjust history of modernity, or of industrial and post-industrial capitalism. It did not herald a qualitatively new age, but a glimpse of realisation, a sometimes-critical coming to terms with the limits of modernity itself (which is no small deal). Postmodernity, further, was demonstrated to be not a universal project of culture, but a specifically North American phenomenon; even if it was global in its manifestations, it was still American-centric. Jameson associated it with expansion of "a whole new wave of American military and economic domination throughout the world" (1991: 5) externally, and a closed-in consumer culture internally, "an immense dilation of its sphere (the sphere of commodities)" (1991: x).

Contemporaneity opens up an odd development, partly anticipated and partly a surprise. Notable in the widespread proliferation of the term "contemporary" is the severing of reference to modernity and modern times that was once so crucial to conceiving of Western civilisation's place—its sense of self as a mere production of otherness. This might be quite simply how the contemporary functions as well. Against the concepts of the modern and the postmodern, which were seen as linked to the commitment (or not) to a project of civilisation (cruelly stamping out otherness), contemporaneity might be best characterised not as a lack that must be overcome (in a Hegelian or Heideggerian sense) but as an enigma that remains perpetually unresolved (in Mario Perniola's sense). This suggests very different ontological and ideological makeups to the contemporary as opposed to the modern and the postmodern; the former may simply be in a period of immaturity—to be followed by something like a "proper" modernity, post-European and post-global—while the later retain their differences.

In high modernity, life was still organised into two distinct temporalities: the city and the countryside. In the contemporary, major technologies such as cyberspace—which William Gibson famously defined as a "consensual hallucination experienced daily by billions of legitimate operators, in every nation … . A graphic representation of data abstracted from the banks of every computer in the human system. Unthinkable complexity" (2001: 67)—help to obliterate temporal lagging, and remake the most rural lands in the image of the urban. The once-distinct temporalities of day and night are also eroding. These erosions have had and will continue to effect profound changes within architecture and the way we live. Indeed, a precondition for the culture of contemporaneity is that the project and its old city centres, such as Petersburg, Paris, and New York—the modernist cities named by Marshall Berman in *All That is Solid Melts into Air: The Experience of Modernity* (a text that is now historical and classic in its own right)—no longer have the same kind of authoritative influence over today's narratives of aesthetic development, temporality, and difference. (Berman specified New York for the Robert Moses project, Paris for George Eugene Haussmann's boulevards, and Petersburg for Russia's distorted modernisation: a flash forward to what became the late twentieth century's so-called Third Worlds.) Further, the instituting of the contemporary appears as the final, hegemonic co-optation of the idea, well known from critical theory, that history and aesthetics have no intrinsic narrative of development of the sort that Hegel (in the nineteenth century) and, later, Martin Heidegger (in the twentieth) wanted to introduce.

My suggestion in such a situation as the potential exhaustion of both modernity and postmodernity turns on a characterisation of Perniola's. Modernity was relatively planned and directed, postmodernity continued in critical reference to the admittedly failed plan and direction of modernity, but contemporaneity has abandoned the notion of modern life as one lived within a project centred around realising any model of a future. In fact, we generally now see such attempts at realisation, and even modelling itself, as very dangerous indeed. The enigma, as Perniola has described it, goes beyond the society of the spectacle as conceived by Guy Debord (Perniola 1995: 10–12). The society of the spectacle was characterised not by *concentration* as in Stalinist Russia or Nazi Germany, but by *diffuseness*, as in that developed within the post-World War Two United States. The characterisation of the contemporary as an enigma that is not bound to be solved adds clarity and permits imagination to that otherwise contentless, massively deployed cultural category that is so unlike historical modernity. Modernity posited a lack within the present and a coming, messianic future object, and postmodernity constituted a narrative critique whose project was one of departing from the treacherous forward momentum of modernity at all cost. The great distance is the critical one: the contemporary is not, by default, a critical category, but modernity and postmodernity were.

The expansion of the New York MoMA was exemplary of a certain aspect of the contemporary cultural condition, namely, centred around expensive and seemingly limitless extension, but in the absence of a coherent project—at least, in the absence of what modernism and postmodernism would have grasped as a coherent project (whether or not the object was to expound and promote or critique and denigrate). Yoshio Taniguchi's expansion was held to illustrate an enigmatic condition; the contemporary, which was decadently deployed at the esteemed modernist headquarters, both exceeds the modern and *includes* the postmodern, but is not limited to it. By contrast, "the contemporary" is extraordinarily undisciplined; it allows the postmodern to exist alongside a fresh version of the high modern. For this reason, it feels emptied of content, contradictory, and disallowed of the modern's critique of the commodity, which the museum promotes again at a higher level, both in the expanded shop and in the individual exhibits that elevate once-critical objects and paintings to the status almost of crown jewels. Very eerily, the new minimalism of Taniguchi speaks to the most radical of the aesthetic avant-gardes. Dada has become the institution's financial-architectural Unconscious; in contemporaneity, Dada, once critical, has become the artistic equivalent of the architects such as Koolhaas—who proclaim an autonomy from the system of global capitalism—but are really the willing playthings of the élites.

The biggest orgies of the eternal present are to be found in architecture, where resources, people, and capital alike are all exhausted in the same mega-projects: projects that cannot sensibly be argued to be in keeping with the ethical visions of modernism, and to some critical extent, with postmodernism (which at least contained a critique of the excesses and failures of modernism as a project). The post-ethical architectural projects in the US, China, and especially the UAE, are the ultimate signs of a modernity that has lost its belief in building a relationship with the future and, in turn, a relationship to the globalised present. Its relationship is not one of long-term goals in the face of the impending disasters of the new century—the great hangovers of war and global warming that we have collectively inherited from an aggressive and imperial modernity and two centuries of coal and oil-driven industrialism and, later, consumption—but of investment in compensatory fantasy environments and a level of luxurious living that were barely thinkable, and perhaps not desirable, within first-wave European modernity.

Dubai is particularly disturbing in the way that its architecture reveals a speed and deployment of resources on a scale unseen in modernism's history, yet mere excess and abundance are its driving motivations in the face of a planet that is well-aware of its mass urban impoverishments (as outlined by Mike Davis) and multiple narratives of the end of oil and resources. Dubai might be an incredible archaeological find for the socialist historians of the future: the ultimate sign of the orgiastic *dénouement* of global capitalist civilisation in the creation of unsustainable fantasy lands for an élite that lives off virtually feudal divisions of labour.

Unlike in modernity and postmodernity, we are trained to not expect to go beyond contemporaneity. It is naturalised as the absolute of our cultural experience and as the highest form of cultural awareness that we might have. The accompanying attitudes of modernity and postmodernity gave us something to do. Koolhaas' colleague, Sze Tsung Leong, has suggested that "in the end, there will be little else for us to do but shop" is surely a recognition of an achieved pseudo-Utopia of the present, made possible by late capitalism and the maintenance of a system that has luxury and consumption on the inside and forced labour and impoverishment on the outside (Jameson 2003: 77). The "future" undergoes a radical reduction in such a circumstance, in which power is held in the hands of a small élite, and might only henceforth be experienced in the form of an excitement about the money to be made—a short-term, selfish, and ultimately meaningless endeavour.

Within modernity, the key crisis was tradition—the broad effects of the industrial revolution and the rising and falling bourgeois classes across Europe recognised, in Marshall Berman's phrase borrowed from *The Communist Manifesto*, that "all that was solid melted into air", which was especially evident in the new commodity system as analysed by Marx and later the Frankfurt School theorists. Tradition was fragmenting and being discontinued all over the place, and a new society, a faster society, an internationally aspiring system and world market was emerging in its place. Think of the vast colonial structures as much as the risk-ridden triumphs of bourgeois technology (such as the iconic RMS *Titanic*). (A contemporary equivalent might be hinted at in the form of the new safety discourses surrounding the space tourism industry—an industry awaiting a probable blow to its ideology of progress.) According to Ezra Pound, in the modernist present one found indicative objects, temporally advanced creatures that seemed to hint towards a better world: an infinitely progressing world that, through technology and, in the fine arts, the break away from convention and the rise of Abstraction (and geometry as a resource for renewing art), promised everything. It was the Enlightenment manifested finally in terms of a class that valued rationality, efficiency, progress, and the world of tomorrow over the past and tradition, which had been blown to the wind (literally, in the cases of war and revolution). Modernity was, above all—at least, before the blow to progress that was the Great War—an age of excitement, of invention, of speed, and unbelievable technological advance.

Postmodernity sought an end to the excesses of modernity;[1] it was a critical project, but not one based on realising a Utopia. The worst aspects of modernity had been revealed through then-recent European and world history. The Enlightenment, according to the famous critique by Adorno and Horkheimer, had ended in the Holocaust. Zygmunt Bauman's analysis brought their argument to the next level when he argued in *Modernity and the Holocaust* that aspects of modernity that were valued in some parts of the world—rationalism, technology, machinic production, organisation—were as easily put to the uses of atrocity elsewhere. For Bauman, the Holocaust was congruent with the highest modern notions and

---

[1] Nobody likes a technocracy; the characters in the 1965 film *Alphaville* wished to escape theirs, as it were, into some imagined "post"-modernity.

used the same set of modern rationalist ideas and technical advances (such as International Business Machines) of which, elsewhere, Western societies were proud (such as in the United States).

In architecture, a similar line of argument can be drawn. The Corbusian intelligence of functionalism and mass-housing projects, of prefabrication, planning, re-zoning, and the aspiration to some ultimate condition of the machine—the individual building as a machine within the city as machine, and further, the individual human unit as a "machine man" or modular person that locked into the whole functional system—ended up as the realisation, in the worst examples, of a more concrete and perfected alienation. Modernist architects believed in an essentially "thaumaturgic" power of architecture. They acknowledged the power of architecture on the human body, and on populations, but failed to recognise its inherent violence on it. Modern architecture became, as Peter Blake suggested in *Form Follows Fiasco*, a vast Giacommetti machine, producing isolated, withdrawn figures, not fully realised humans, but, as Sartre observed in his 1948 essay on the Swiss sculptor, creatures rendered forever in the distance, in a singular dimension, without middle and foregrounds, at "an absolute distance" (Sartre: 603). Pruitt-Igoe remains the ultimate example of this kind of architecturally enabled and realised state of collective folly. Today, the example can be used to project an image of the future of architecture that is dangerous and undesirable.

That was the postmodern critique, at least part of it. If modernity saw crisis in tradition, the postmoderns saw the *tradition of modernity* itself in crisis. This had to be radically revised. The artists, architects, and cultural theorists during this time of rapid turnaround of received "modern" ideas and practices provide us with the best access to the problems and their supposed solutions. The postmoderns sought a Kantian exit from the excesses of modernity, which, through the identification of what Wolf Schafer called the "modernity syndrome", understood its product—a whole philosophy of life and progress—to be universal. This proved incredibly difficult, or even just plain wrong, especially as it justified a continuation of the colonised peoples of the world.

The postmodernists were a confluence of individuals from various generations in a *moment* of strong realisation in the post-war and Cold War eras who collectively sought plurality, difference, and multiplicity as high ideals, implicit critiques, and modes of radical exit from what had become the horrors of the modern universal rationality—controlled by the few. The philosophical notion of difference from the 1960s eventually saw its institutionalisation as multiculturalism in the 1990s—an ideology that might be seen to function to conceal its own internal disorders. In architecture, a wide embrace of popular vernaculars, appropriation of non-architectural forms, and a new appreciation for fun, nostalgia, and play came to offer a way out of the Modern Movement and Corbusian rule. Significantly, it was North American; Las Vegas was hailed as the Utopia of post-Modern urban life, of floating signs and a multi-directional infantilisation of the subject. (The exploitative industries of gambling and sex, it might be noted, did not enter into Venturi and Scott-Brown's analysis, which was still operating from within a mode of architectural purism.) Bruce Bégout updates Venturi and Scott-Brown for "the contemporary" where the city is analysed as a bleak non-city prototype for current urbanity everywhere: "no man's land, waste ground, non-place, ghost town, urban simulacrum, nowhere city, etc. For us it is Zeropolis ... the degree zero city of urbanity, of architecture and culture, the degree zero city of sociability, art and ideas" (Bégout: 22).

The so-called "contemporary" paradigm is often presented, and presents itself, as offering an exit—however temporary or provisional—from the cultural framework of a rigid and authoritarian modernism (long outmoded) and a postmodernism that itself has become historical (banished to the dustbin of the 1980s and 1990s). The category of "the contemporary" does not fail, and cannot fail, unless it is reloaded with content and a destination. Alain Badiou's complaint about contemporary art was: "It says: 'Everything is possible', which is also to say that nothing is" (2006: 148). Much of the aggressive cultural production of the present indicates the new scale of resources (at their moment of crisis) and the mobilisation of people—whether labour forces or consumers—that have become achievable but are still directed en masse into what Adolf Loos pejoratively called the ornamental. An alternative would redirect these profound abilities to changing the very substance of a collective life that will not leap centuries ahead of itself into a brighter future, as long as it refuses the difficult path of experimenting with the dangers of planning and commitment (that need not necessarily be authoritarian), and the attempt to resolve the false sense of the eternal experienced collectively within a present that increasingly has no use for its past except as a warehouse of accumulated artefacts to be auctioned.

# References

Adamson, Glenn, and Jane Pavitt. 2011. "Curators' Foreword." In *Postmodernism: Style and Subversion, 1970-1990*, eds. Glenn Adamson and Jane Pavitt. London: V&A Publishing.

Adorno, Theodor, and Max Horkheimer. 1979. *Dialectic of Enlightenment*, trans. John Cumming. London: Verso.

Alderman, Liz. 2010. "After Crisis, Dubai Keeps Building, but Soberly." *The New York Times*, September 29, http://www.nytimes.com/2010/09/30/business/global/30dubai.html.

AMO. 2004. "CCTV." In *Content*, eds. Rem Koolhaas and Brian McGetrick, 489. Koln: Taschen.

Augé, Marc. 1999. *An Anthropology for Contemporaneous Worlds*, trans. Amy Jacobs. Stanford: Stanford University Press.

Badiou, Alain. 2006. *Polemics*, trans. Steve Corcoran. London: Verso.

---. 2007. *The Century*, trans. Alberto Toscano. London: Polity.

Ballard, J.G. 1975. *High-Rise*. London: Vintage.

Barthes, Roland. 1973. *Mythologies*, trans. Annette Levers.

London: Paladin.

Baudelaire, Charles. 1995. "The Painter of Modern Life." In *The Painter of Modern Life and Other Essays*, trans. J. Mayne, 1–41. New York: Phaidon.

Bauman, Zygmunt. 1989. *Modernity and the Holocaust*. Cambridge: Polity.

---. 2002. "The 20th Century: An End or a Beginning?" *Thesis Eleven* 70: 15–25.

Bégout, Bruce. 2003. *Zeropolis: The Experience of Las Vegas*, trans. Liz Heron. London: Reaktion Books.

Benjamin, Walter. 1999. *The Arcades Project*, trans. Howard Eiland and Kevin McLaughlin. Cambridge: Belknap.

Berman, Marshall. 1988. *All That is Solid Melts into Air: The Experience of Modernity*. Harmondsworth: Penguin.

Birkholz, Knut. 2006. "CCTV or: Architecture Meets Life." Graz Architecture Magazine 03: 170–185.

Birmingham, Elizabeth. 1999. "Reframing the Ruins: Pruitt Igoe, Structural Racism, and African American Rhetoric as a Space for Cultural Critique." *Western Journal of Communication* 16.3: 291–309.

Blake, Peter. 1977. *Form Follows Fiasco: Why Modern Architecture Hasn't Worked*. Boston: Little Brown.

Bloch, Ernst. 1991. *Heritage of Our Times*, trans. Neville and Stephen Plaice. Cambridge, UK: Polity.

Bockris, Victor. 1989. *The Life and Death of Andy Warhol*. New York: Bantam.

Bouman, Ole, Mitra Khoubrou, and Rem Koolhaas, eds. 2007. *Al Manakh: Dubai Guide–Gulf Survey–Global Agenda*. Amsterdam: Archis.

Brenson, Michael. 2002. *The Guggenheim, Corporate Pluralism, and the Future of the Corporate Museum*. New York: Vera List Center for Art and Politics.

Breton, André. 1972. *Manifestoes of Surrealism*, trans. Richard Seaver and Helen R. Lane. Ann Arbor: University of Michigan Press.

Buck-Morss, Susan. 2000. *Dreamworld and Catastrophe: The Passing of Mass Utopia in East and West*. Cambridge, MA: M.I.T. Press.

Calinescu, Matei. 1987. *The Five Faces of Modernity: Modernism, Avant-Garde, Decadence, Kitsch, Postmodernism.* Durham: Duke University Press.

Chavez, Hugo. 2011. "We are Rising Up Against the Empire". In *Infamous speeches: From Robespierre to Osama bin Laden,* ed. Bob Blaisdell, 225–232. Mineola, NY: Dover Publications.

Chomsky, Noam. 2003. *Hegemony or Survival: America's Quest for Global Dominance.* Crow's Nest: Allen and Unwin.

Chung, Chuihua Judy, Rem Koolhaas, Jeffrey Inaba, and Sze Tsung Leong, eds. 2001. *Great Leap Forward.* Taschen: Köln.

Danto, Arthur C. 1997. *After the End of Art: Contemporary Art and the Pale of History.* New Jersey: Princeton University Press.

---. 2013. *What Art Is.* New Haven: Yale University Press.

Davidson, Cynthia. 2005. "MoMA Goes Modern...Again." *Log* 4: 97–102.

Davis, Mike. 2004. "Planet of Slums." *New Left Review* 26: March-April.

---. 2006. "Fear and Money in Dubai." *New Left Review* 41 (September-October): 47–68; http://newleftreview.org/II/41/mike-davis-fear-and-money-in-dubai.

Debord, Guy. 1970. *Society of the Spectacle.* Detroit: Black and Red.

De Graaf, Reinier and Rem Koolhaas. 2004. "€-conography: How to undo Europe's Iconographic Deficit?" In *Content,* ed. Brendan McGetrick, 376–389. New York: Taschen.

Derrida, Jacques. 1994. *The Specters of Marx: The State of the Debt, the Work of Mourning, and the New International,* trans. Peggy Kamuf. New York: Routledge.

Elderfield, John, ed. 1998. *Imagining the Future of The Museum of Modern Art.* New York: Museum of Modern Art.

Enwezor, Okwui. 2003. "Terminal Modernity: Rem Koolhaas' Discourse on Entropy." In *What is OMA: Considering Rem Koolhaas and the Office for Metropolitan Architecture,* ed. Veronique Patteeuw, 103–119. Rotterdam: Netherlands

Architecture Institute.

Fasulo, Linda. 2004. *An Insider's Guide to the UN*. New Haven: Yale University Press.

Foster, Hal. 1996. *The Return of the Real: The Avant-Garde at the End of the Century*. Cambridge: M.I.T. Press.

---. 2003. *Design and Crime (and Other Diatribes)*. London: Verso.

---. 2004. "It's Modern but is it Contemporary?" *London Review of Books* 26.24 (December 16): 23–25.

---. 2011. *The Art-Architecture Complex*. London: Verso.

Foucault, Michel. 1990. *The History of Sexuality: Volume I: An Introduction*, trans. Robert Hurley. New York: Vintage.

---. 1991. "Nietzsche, Genealogy, History." In *The Foucault Reader*, ed. Paul Rainbow, 76–100. New York: Penguin.

---. 1994. *The Order of Things: An Archaeology of the Human Sciences*. New York: Vintage.

Fraser, Murray. 2007. "Beyond Koolhaas." In *Critical Architecture*, eds. Jane Rendell, Jonathon Hill, Murray Fraser, and Mark Dorrian, 332–334. London: Routledge.

Friedman, Thomas L. 2005. *The World is Flat: A Brief History of the Twenty-first Century*. London: Penguin.

Gibson, William. 2001. *Neuromancer*. London: Voyager.

---. 2007. *Spook Country*. London: Viking.

Gill, A.A. 2011. "Dubai on Empty." *Vanity Fair*, April, http://www.vanityfair.com/culture/features/2011/04/dubai-201104.

Goldberger, Paul. 1976. "Modern Museum's Plan for Apartments." *The New York Times*, August 17, 7.

Grosz, Elizabeth. 2000. *Architecture from the Outside*. Cambridge: M.I.T. Press.

Groys, Boris. 2002. "The Loneliness of the Project." In *New York Magazine of Contemporary Art and Theory* 1.1: [n.p].

---. 2008 "The Topology of Contemporary Art." In *Antinomies of Art and Culture: Modernity, Postmodernity, and Contemporaneity*, eds. Terry Smith, Okwui Enwezor, and Nancy Condee, 71–80. Durham: Duke University Press.

---. 2010. "Comrades of Time." In *What is Contemporary Art?*, eds. Julieta Aranda, Brian Kuan Wood, and Anton

Vidokle, 22–39. Berlin: Sternberg.

Guilbaut, Serge. 1985. *How New York Stole the Idea of Modern Art: Abstract Expressionism, Freedom, and the Cold War*, trans. Arthur Goldhammer. Chicago: University of Chicago Press.

Habermas, Jürgen. 1983. "Modernity: An Incomplete Project," trans. Seyla Ben-Habib. In *The Anti Aesthetic: Essays on Postmodern Culture*, ed. Hal Foster, 3–15. Port Townsend: Bay Press.

Hatherlay, Owen. *The New Ruins of Great Britain*. London: Verso, 2010.

Heidegger, Martin. 1977. "The Age of the World Picture." In *The Question Concerning Technology and Other Essays*, trans. William Lovitt, 115–154. New York: Harper and Row.

Hitchcock, Henry-Russell and Phillip Johnson. 1997. *The International Style*. New York: W.W. Norton.

Hoover, Paul, ed. 1994. *Postmodern American Poetry: A Norton Anthology*. New York: W.W. Norton.

Huelsenbeck, Richard. 1998. "What is Dadaism and What Does it Mean for Germany?" In *Art In Theory: An Anthology of Changing Ideas*, eds. Charles Harrison and Paul Wood, 256–257. Oxford: Blackwell.

Huyssen, Andreas. 1995. *Twilight Memories: Marking Time in a Culture of Amnesia*. New York: Routledge.

Irr, Caren and Ian Buchanan, eds. 2006. *On Jameson: From Postmodernism to Globalisation*. Albany: State University of New York Press.

Izenor, Steven and David Dashiell. 1990. "Relearning from Las Vegas." *Architecture* 79.10: 46–51.

Jameson, Fredric. 1984. "Foreword." In Jean-François Lyotard, *The Postmodern Condition: A Report on Knowledge*, vii–xxi. Manchester: Manchester University Press.

---. 1991. *Postmodernism, or, The Cultural Logic of Late Capitalism*. London: Verso.

---. 1996. *The Political Unconscious: Narrative as a Socially Symbolic Act*. New York: Routledge.

---. 2000a. "Globalisation and Political Strategy." *New Left Review* 4 (July-August): 49–68.

---. 2000b. "Cognitive Mapping." In *The Jameson Reader*, eds. Michael Hardt and Kathi Weeks, 277–287. New York: Routledge.

---. 2002. *A Singular Modernity: Essay on the Ontology of the Present*. London: Verso.

---. 2003. "Future City." *New Left Review* 21 (May-June): 65–79.

---. 2005. *Archaeologies of the Future: The Desire Called Utopia and Other Science Fictions*. London: Verso.

Jauss, Hans Robert. 2005. "Modernity and Literary Tradition," trans. C. Thorne. *Critical Inquiry* 31 (Winter): 329–364.

Jencks, Charles. 1981. *The Language of Post-Modern Architecture*. London: Academy Editions.

Johnson, Philip. 1988. "Preface." In *Deconstructivist Architecture*, eds. Philip Johnson and Mark Wigley. New York: The Museum of Modern Art.

Kafka, Franz. 1981. *Amerika*, trans. Willa and Edwin Muir. London: Penguin.

Kant, Immanuel. 1996. "An Answer to the Question: What Is Enlightenment?" In *What Is Enlightenment? Eighteenth Century Answers and Twentieth-Century Questions*, ed. James Schmidt, 58–64. Berkeley: University of California Press.

Kantor, Sybil Gordon. 2002. *Alfred H. Barr, Jr. and the Intellectual Origins of the Museum of Modern Art*. Cambridge: M.I.T. Press.

Katodrytis, George. 2005. "Metropolitan Dubai and the Rise of Architectural Fantasy." *Bidoun* 4 (Spring): http://www.bidoun.org/magazine/04-emirates-now/metropolitan-dubai-and-the-rise-of-architectural-fantasy-by-george-katodrytis/.

Kimmelman, Michael. 2004. "The Thoroughly Modernised Modern." *The New York Times*, November 19, 35–37.

Koolhaas, Rem. 1994. *Delirious New York: A Retroactive Manifesto for Manhattan*. New York: Monacelli.

---. 2004a. "Content." In *Content*, ed. Brendan McGetrick, 20–

21. Koln: Taschen.
---. 2004b. "Junkspace." In *Content*, ed. Brendan McGetrick, 162–171. Koln: Taschen.
---. 2004c. "MoMA Charette." In *Content*, ed. Brendan McGetrick, 190–197. Koln: Taschen.
---. 2004d. "Utopia Station." In *Content*, ed. Brendan McGetrick 393–395. Koln: Taschen.
---. 2004e. "White Briefs Against Filth: The Waning Power of New York." In *Content*, ed. Brendan McGetrick, 236–239. New York: Taschen.
---. 2004f. "Post-modern engineering?" In *Content*, ed. Brendan McGetrick, 515. New York: Taschen.
---. 2007a. "Last Chance?" In Bouman, Khoubrou, and Koolhas, eds., *Al Manakh*, 7.
---. 2007b. "Frontline." In Bouman, Khoubrou, and Koolhas, eds., *Al Manakh*, 194-195.
Krauss, Rosalind. 1999. *'A Voyage on the North Sea': Art in the Age of the Post-Medium Condition.* London: Thames and Hudson.
Kuspit, Donald. 2004a. *The End of Art.* Cambridge: Cambridge University Press.
---. 2005. "The Contemporary and the Historical." *Artnet*: http://www.artnet.com/Magazine/features/kuspit/kuspit4-14-05.asp.
La Cecla, Franco. 2012. *Against Architecture*, trans. Mairin O'Mahony. Oakland, CA: PM Press.
Lahiji, Nadir. 2004. "Une Architecture Autre? Architecture in a Time of Terror." *Architectural Theory Review* 9.2: 1–16.
Le Corbusier. 1971. *The City of Tomorrow and Its Planning*, trans. Frederick Etchells. London: Architectural Press.
---. 1986. *Towards a New Architecture*, trans. F. Etchells. Mineola, NY: Dover.
Lefebvre, Henri. 1995. *Introduction to Modernity: Twelve Preludes September 1959-May 1961*, trans. John Moore. London: Verso.
Lewis, Wyndham. 1954. *Demon of Progress in the Arts.* London: Methuen.
Louchheim, Aline B. 1948. "'Modern' or 'Contemporary'

Words or Meanings?" *The New York Times*, June 27, Section 2: 8.
Loughery, John. 2001. "The Future of Museums: The Guggenheim, MoMA, and the Tate Modern." *The Hudson Review* LIII. 4 (Winter): 631–38.
Lowry, Glen D. 2005. *The New Museum of Modern Art*. New York: Museum of Modern Art.
Lynch, Kevin. 1960. *The Image of the City*. Cambridge, MA: M.I.T. Press.
Lyotard, Jean-François. 2004. *The Postmodern Condition: A Report on Knowledge*, trans. Geoffery Bennington and Brian Massumi. Manchester: Manchester University Press.
Mandel, Ernest. 1978. *Late Capitalism*, trans. Joris De Bres. London: Verso.
Marx, Karl. 1983. *The Portable Karl Marx*, trans. Eugene Kamenka. Harmondsworth: Penguin.
Mau, Bruce and Rem Koolhaas, eds. 1998. *S, M, L, XL: Office for Metropolitan Architecture*. New York: Monacelli.
Mitchell, William J. 2005. "Less is More is Back." *Placing Words: Symbols, Space, and the City*, 172–75. Cambridge: M.I.T. Press.
Moretti, Franco. 2000. "MoMA2000: The Capitulation." *New Left Review* 4 (July-August): 98-102; http://newleftreview.org/II/4/franco-moretti-moma-2000-the-capitulation.
Muschamp, Herbert. 1997. "Make the Modern Modern?" *The New York Times*, June 15, http://partners.nytimes.com/library/magazine/home/20000709mag-muschamp.8.html.
Myers, Tracy. 2004. "'The Possibility of Exception': Lebbeus Woods's Passionate Provocations." In *Lebbeus Woods: Experimental Architecture*, eds. Tracy Myers, Lebbeus Woods, and Karsten Harries. Pittsburgh: Carnegie Museum of Art.
Nietzsche, Friedrich. 1996. *On the Genealogy of Morals*, trans. Douglas Smith. Oxford: Oxford University Press.
---. 1998. *Beyond Good and Evil: Prelude to a Philosophy of the Future*, trans. Marion Faber. New York: Oxford University Press.
Ogbechie, Sylvester Okwunodu. 2008. "The Perils of Unilateral Power: Neomodernist Metaphors and the New Global

Order." In *Antinomies of Art and Culture: Modernity, Postmodernity, and Contemporaneity*, eds. Terry Smith, Okwui Enwezor, and Nancy Condee, 165–186. Durham: Duke University Press.

Osbourne, Peter. 1995. *The Politics of Time: Modernity and Avant-Garde*. London: Verso.

Ouroussoff, Nicholai. 2007. "Next to MoMA, a Tower Will Reach for the Stars." *The New York Times*, November 15, http://www.nytimes.com/2007/11/15/arts/design/15arch.html.

Perniola, Mario. 1995. *Enigmas: The Egyptian Moment in Society and Art*, trans. Christopher Woodall. London: Verso.

Perloff, Marjorie. 2002. *21st-Century Modernism: The "New" Poetics*. Oxford: Blackwell.

Poggioli, Renato. 1968. *The Theory of the Avant-Garde*, trans. Gerald Fitzgerald. London: Belknap.

Pound, Ezra. 1960. *ABC of Reading*. London: Faber and Faber.

Rajchman, John. 2003. "Unhappy Returns: Writing the '80s Post-modernism." *Artforum International* 41.8 (April).

Saltz, Jerry. 2005a. "A Modest Proposal." *Village Voice*, January 18, http://www.villagevoice.com/2005-01-18/art/a-modest-proposal/.

---. 2005b. "One Year After." *Village Voice*, November 8, http://www.villagevoice.com/2005-11-08/art/one-year-after/.

Sartre, Jean-Paul. 1948. "The Search for the Absolute." In *Art in Theory: An Anthology of Changing Ideas*, eds. Charles Harrison and Paul Wood, 599–604. Oxford: Blackwell.

Saul, John Ralston. 2005. *The Collapse of Globalism: and the Reinvention of the World*. London: Penguin.

Schafer, Wolf. 2004. "Global History and the Present Time." In *Wiring Prometheus: Globalisation, History and Technology*, eds. Peter Lyth and Helmuth Trischler, 103–125. Denmark: Aarhus University Press.

Scholes, Robert. 2006. *Paradoxy of Modernism*. New Haven: Yale University Press.

Smith, Douglas. 1996. "Introduction." In Friedrich Nietzsche, *On the Genealogy of Morals*, vii-xxi. Oxford: Oxford University Press.

Smith, Terry. 2001. *Contemporary Art, Contemporaneity and Art to Come.* Sydney: Art Space.

---. 2005. "Manhattan is Modern, but not contemporary, Again." *Art Monthly Australia* 178 (April): 3-9.

---. 2006a. "Contemporary Art and Contemporaneity." *Critical Inquiry* 32.4 (Summer): 681-707.

---. 2006b. *The Architecture of Aftermath.* Chicago: University of Chicago Press.

---. 2006c. "World Picturing in Contemporary Art: Iconogeographic Turning." *Australian and New Zealand Journal of Art* 7.1: 24-46.

---. 2008. "Introduction: The Contemporaneity Question." In *Antinomies of Art and Culture: Modernity, Postmodernity, and Contemporaneity*, eds. Terry Smith, Okwui Enwezor, and Nancy Condee, 1-16. Durham: Duke University Press.

Stallabrass, Julian. 1999. *High Art Lite: British Art in the 1990s.* London: Verso.

---. 2004. *Art Incorporated: The Story of Contemporary Art.* Oxford: Oxford University Press.

Sterling, Bruce. 1993. "A Short History of the Internet." *The Magazine of Fantasy and Science Fiction*, February, https://w2.eff.org/Net_culture/internet_sterling.history.txt.

---. 2003. "A User's Guide to AMO." In *What is OMA: Considering Rem Koolhaas and the Office for Metropolitan Architecture*, ed. Veronique Patteeuw, 167-76. Rotterdam: Netherlands Architecture Institute.

Taylor, Jennifer. 2007. Unpublished lecture given at Royal Australian Institute of Architects, July, Potts Point, Sydney.

Thompson, Don. 2008. *The $12 Million Stuffed Shark: The Curious Economics of Art and Auction Houses.* London: Aurum.

UN-HABITAT. 2004. "Press Release on the Conclusion of the UN-Habitat Symposium on Housing and Urban Development: Decade of Shelter for All in Iraq." http://www.docstoc.com/docs/document-preview.aspx?doc_id=30476440.

Updike, John. 2004. "Invisible Cathedral: A Walk Through

the New Modern." *The New Yorker*, November 15, http://www.newyorker.com/magazine/2004/11/15/invisible-cathedral.

Varnedoe, Kirk. 2001. "Introduction." *Modern Contemporary: Art Since 1980 at MoMA*. New York: Museum of Modern Art.

Venturi, Robert, Denise Scott Brown, and Steven Izenor, eds. 1977. *Learning From Las Vegas: The Forgotten Symbolism of Architectural Form*. Cambridge: M.I.T. Press.

Vidler, Anthony. 2004. "Architecture's Expanded Field: Finding Inspiration in Jellyfish and Geopolitics." *Artforum International* 42.8.

Virilio, Paul. 2003. *Art and Fear*, trans. Julie Rose. London: Continuum.

Von Hoffman, Alexander. 2006. "Why They Built the Pruitt Igoe Project." Joint Center for Housing Studies at Harvard University, http://www.soc.iastate.edu/sapp/PruittIgoe.html.

Wallach, Alan. 1992. "The Museum of Modern Art: The Past's Future." *Journal of Design History* 5.3: 207–215.

Wark, McKenzie. 2008. "The Gift Shop at the End of History." In *Antinomies of Art and Culture: Modernity, Postmodernity, and Contemporaneity*, eds. Terry Smith, Okwui Enwezor, and Nancy Condee, 345–362. Durham: Duke University Press.

Williams, Raymond. 1983. "The Estranging Language of Post-Modernism." *New Society* 16 (June): 439–440.

Werner, Paul. 2005. *Museum, Inc: Inside the Global Art World*. Chicago: Prickly Paradigm Press.

Westwood, Matthew. 2007. "Donations Bring MCA Upgrade Closer." *The Australian*, August 31.

Woods, Lebbeus. 1992. *Anarchitecture: Architecture is a Political Act*. New York: St. Martin's.

---. 1993. *War and Architecture*. New York: Princeton University Press.

---. 2004a. *The Storm and the Fall*. New York: Princeton University Press.

---. 2004b. "Taking on Risk: Nine Experimental Scenarios." In *Lebbeus Woods: Experimental Architecture*, ed. Tracy Myers, 24–37. Pittsburgh: Carnegie Museum of Art.

Yamasaki, Minoru. 1979. *A Life in Architecture.* New York: Weatherhill.

# Acknowledgments

This book is very much the work of an ongoing discussion in which many people have been involved at various stages. My sincerest thanks are due to those who read the manuscript, or sections of it, took the time to comment, and offered their thoughts and criticisms: Nick Mansfield, Terry Smith, Bart Verschaffel, Gevork Hartoonian, Ian Buchanan, Don Sillence, Chris AC, Rohan Pearce, Rowan Tulloch, Darien Jane Hamilton, Ben de Nardi, Karen Johnson, Léopold Lambert, Franco La Cecla, and Mary McCormick.

Thank you as well to Shua Garfield, Troy Emery, Sarah Hodgetts, David Adlam, Debra Fast, Marita Bullock, Susan Krieg, Nils Crompton, and Sara Fernandes. Thanks also to Justin Devlin, Lara Palombo, Elaine Laforteza, and staff and students at Macquarie City Campus.

Thanks to Adolfo Natalini for permission to use Superstudio's art on the cover, to Diletta Pantani for invaluable assistance, and Katherine Johnson for the layout of the cover design.

Thanks are also due to Eileen A. Joy of punctum for being such a pleasure to work with on publishing this volume.

Early pieces appeared in *Architectural Theory Review* (vol. 12, no. 1: 2007) and *Colloquy* (vol. 14: 2007). "Koolhaas in Beijing," in Chapter 4, slightly altered, appeared in the book *Architecture, Disciplinarity and the Arts*, edited by John Macarthur and Andrew Leach (Gent: A&S, 2008).

This book is dedicated to my parents, G.L. Johnson[†] and Judith E.P. Johnson.

www.ingramcontent.com/pod-product-compliance
Lightning Source LLC
Chambersburg PA
CBHW072043160426
43197CB00014B/2609